South of Heaven

South of Heaven

My year in Afghanistan

Daniel Flores

with Sandra Parisi Kilisz

iUniverse, Inc.
Bloomington

South of Heaven
My year in Afghanistan

iUniverse books may be ordered through booksellers or by contacting:

iUniverse
1663 Liberty Drive
Bloomington, IN 47403
www.iuniverse.com
1-800-Authors (1-800-288-4677)

ISBN: 978-1-4620-2438-4 (sc)
ISBN: 978-1-4620-2437-7 (dj)
ISBN: 978-1-4620-2436-0 (ebk)

Library of Congress Control Number: 2011908519

Printed in the United States of America

iUniverse rev. date: 07/12/2011

Contents

Dedicated to my Mom and Dad.

Thank you for your prayers.

Acknowledgements

First and foremost, I thank God and Jesus Christ for everything I have.

I took hundreds of pictures, kept a daily log, had family save all my emails, and filmed hours of videos, all of which I used as reference in writing this memoir. I wanted to ensure that I could look back at this part of my life and remember everything that happened for generations to come.

I only took a few pictures of my time on active duty, and I wish I had taken so many more.

This project started out as notes I was going to put with my pictures and videos to explain each one. It was going to be a memoir that my children's children could look back on and see what I had done in this war. This project was never intended to be published.

Thanks to Sandra for suggesting I write a book. Her inspiration and drive pushed me to make this a book for more than just family and close friends.

Kim and Chris Mihok; I know God planned our meeting that snowy day for a specific reason. Kimi listened to my project and inspired me to "get the word out". After listening to me describe one of my missions and then showing them the video clip that went along with the story, they knew that every American needed to know what the news media would never say, and to inspire Americans with this memoir.

Most of all, I need to thank my wife and children for putting up with me during the pursuit of this project and for being there for me when I wanted to give up.

This Battle is over,

As I fly away,

A life taken,

A life saved,

Forever in my mind

How will this stay.

<u>Prologue</u>

I asked my daughter what she thought about her father going to war. With an answer well beyond her 10 years of age, she said, "Dad I know you're going to be O.K. You're the best at what you do, and God told me he will take care of you, so I'm not worried". One thing I've learned as a parent is that kids are smarter than most adults give them credit for.

Her answer left me speechless. I had expected her to start crying, or run off to her room and slam the door closed because she did not want to talk about the inevitable. Instead, we talked about what to expect while I was gone. I listened to her tell me what she thought about the war, and why I had to go. She seemed to fully realize that our country needed me to travel to the other side of the world, to help an oppressed people rebuild their country.

My son took the news pretty hard. Even though he was only 7, he knew the possible consequences of me leaving to go fight the war on terrorism. He understood that there was a chance I would not be coming home. I asked him what his visualization of me going to war was, and I could see it in his eyes before he answered, "You could get killed". I told him, "Yes, I could, but I will be flying in the Apache, and the real war is in Iraq, not in Afghanistan where I am going".

My wife was on pins and needles, trying to keep the household calm, while we both were getting all of the final legal and financial issues taken care of. I signed over a power of attorney to her so she could sign my name to any documents, as need be, and make any legal decisions while I was gone. I purchased home mortgage insurance, to make sure the family wouldn't lose the house if anything happened to me. I purchased an extended warranty on our car, to make sure it was covered if any problems arose. Lastly, we both updated our wills, to make sure the kids were taken care of in case anything happened to either of us.

I had been going over the financial ramifications of this deployment, and crunched the numbers over and over again, in hopes of discovering that I had made a simple math mistake and really wasn't taking a massive pay cut from my civilian job. This deployment was going to hurt, both emotionally and financially.

I reassured my wife and family that, up to this point, the *real war* was actually in Iraq, not in Afghanistan, where I was headed. Family and friends were calling more frequently, hoping to hear that my deployment was canceled; but I had been training for this moment for 19 years, and my selfish little secret was that I really did want to go. I wanted to fly and fight in this foreign place. I had visions of grandeur, of killing Osama Bin Laden myself. I was anxious to get into the action, and get some payback for 9-11.

My main fear was of something happening to my family back in the states while I was away. I wasn't worried about my safety; I was worried about getting a phone call, or an e-mail, telling me that someone was in an accident. I would have no way of getting to them. I constantly told my family that I was okay, and they needed to take care of themselves—so I wouldn't have to worry about them.

It was late 2005. The total casualties in Afghanistan were just barely over one hundred, and the news agencies were publicizing, every day, all of the thousands of American soldiers that were dying in Iraq. There was rarely any mention of there even being a war in Afghanistan. I was actually thinking that it would be a nice flying vacation over a country with a long, deep history. I loved the mountains, and knew that Afghanistan was home to some serious peaks. I was even considering taking my snowboard, and getting some leisure time in!

Little did I know, one year later I would be witness to the Taliban resurgence, lose friends, be locked in a battle for my life against a determined enemy, and be in one of the most notorious and highly-contested valleys in the Hindu Kush, without bullets in my Apache gunship. The final week of my rotation in-country was a true testament to my faith, and to the words my daughter had told me one year prior.

Chapter 1

Storm Brewing

Lisa *When you marry a pilot you have to be willing to take whatever time you can get and get used to him being gone a lot. He was gone a lot before we were married so I was already used to the strange hours, but when I got pregnant, right after his crash, I became more concerned about his absences. I went into labor when he was flying in the Sam Houston forest and I had to wait until he got home before I could go to the hospital. We had a system in place so I could alert him if he was flying. Using my cell phone I sent him a 911 message so he knew that he had to land and get home.*

It was early spring in Southeast Texas, and the battle of the change of seasons was in full swing. There was a looming squall line of severe thunderstorms in the northwest and, several miles away, the night ignited with lightning. A thin layer of clouds had developed at about 1,000 feet over the airport. Looking straight up, you could see the stars overhead; but when you looked out across the sky, you couldn't see above this thin layer.

As an Apache helicopter pilot, I had to remain current and proficient in my skills. I was required to have three take-offs and landings at night, every 90 days, in order to just remain current and be legal to fly. Currency was not the main goal; proficiency was. In order to remain proficient in the art and science of flying, and shooting, in eight tons of high-performance war-fighting machine, I had to fly as often as possible . . . to have it become second-nature and a natural reflex. I had to be able to fly without thinking about the need to hit this pedal, look at that gauge. I basically needed to be "a natural", so I could perform at my best when in battle, and not be worried about the basics of flying. Flight school was over, training was over; this was the real deal.

It was Monday, March 6, 1995, and I was flying the Apache helicopter in the late hours of the evening. My good friend and co-pilot, Johnny, and I had been given orders to fly six more hours of Night Vision System (NVS) time, before we would meet all the prerequisites to shoot live ammunition. NVS is the primary means of flying the Apache at night. It uses strictly infrared energy, so it doesn't need any light at all; it only detects heat. The integrated sight system basically tells the aircraft where my head/vision is pointed, so it can move the infrared camera and weapons in the same direction. The image is projected onto a small Helmet Display Unit (HDU), which is an eye-piece over the right eye.

We were preparing for the live-fire gunnery which we were to conduct in a few weeks. A gunnery is required by the Army, in order to maintain currency and proficiency on the weapons of the Apache. It is basically a shooting range where ammunition can be fired, but not at live targets. Real ammo is used, but they aren't combat loads; so they don't explode like the real thing. We had already flown four hours of NVS time, performing various gunnery scenarios in our training area over East Texas National Forest land, and had returned to our home base to refuel and try to finish up the rest of the flight time, as needed. Earlier that day, I had done a full eight-hour shift at my civilian job as a petrochemical worker, before making the long drive to fly this mission. I was not looking forward to finishing up the flight, then making the long drive home, where I would try to get some sleep, before getting up early the next morning and doing both jobs all over again. However, that was the life of a Warrant Officer flying attack helicopters in the Army reserves. I was young, and it was the hottest attack helicopter in the world, and someone was actually paying me to fly! This left little room for me to complain.

My wife had expressed concerns about my safety while flying helicopters and airplanes in pursuit of this great aviation dream-job; but I would reassure her by describing all of the safety equipment that was incorporated into the aircraft. This discussion would usually turn into a description of how the missiles are capable of defeating any known enemy tank in the world; how the 30mm gun could fire 650 rounds per minute, with each bullet being able to punch through four inches of steel, and kill anything within several feet; or of the vast array of different types of rockets that we could carry, ranging from multipurpose sub-munitions to a Flechette Round, which holds several thousand 2 inch steel nails. They could cut through steel, or the human body, with no problems whatsoever. I would jokingly tell her that, if something were to happen to me, then she would win what we call the "Army Lotto". The Army Lotto is the soldiers' nickname for the Army's life insurance plan for our survivors. If you "maxed out" your elections for life insurance, then your spouse, or whatever beneficiary, would get a huge check of $200,000 to cover the loss of their loved one, who died fighting in defense of our country. The joke was just GUN PILOT bravado coming out of me. I knew that surely nothing could ever hurt me.

After getting more fuel, Johnny and I jumped back in and fired up the aircraft. We both agreed we would stay in the traffic pattern at home base, in order to avoid getting caught in the coming storm. After a few traffic patterns, using our NVS, fatigue was starting to set in. The helicopter can be flown from either the front or back seat. Mission-wise, the pilot-in-command, who does most of the actual flying, is in the back seat and the majority of the shooting is done from the front seat; but, there are controls in both positions, to fly or shoot with. I was on the controls of the aircraft, flying it from the front seat.

Most of our flying is done at speeds much slower than our airplane brethren. We're in a helicopter, and can land vertically if we want; but for emergencies and limited power conditions, we can also make a straight landing, just like an airplane. I was making a right turn, to set myself up for a normal, hovering landing at the approach-end of runway 14, and made my usual radio calls on the local traffic frequency, letting anyone in the area know of my intentions. This airport had no control tower, so it was up to each pilot to announce, to anyone listening, his actions—whether he was landing or taking off, and on which runway.

I was in the traffic pattern for runway 14, looking out to the right of the aircraft to begin my descent, as I approached the end of the runway. We intentionally leave the runway lights off, whenever we are landing on a specific runway; because, when you are using the Night Vision System, they can be distracting. Also, it prevents the newer pilots from cheating, and not relying solely on the NVS. All at once, the radio crackled to life. A Learjet announced that he was on a four-mile final approach, to the same runway I was landing on. I called back on the radio, to make sure that the Learjet knew of my intentions. Johnny got on the radio, and tried to make contact with the Learjet also, with no success. We never heard from the Learjet again.

I suddenly got an uneasy feeling. I was making a standard helicopter approach, at around 40 knots of airspeed. The Learjet was somewhere behind me, doing close to 150 knots. Doing some quick math in my tired brain, I was thinking, "This guy is about to run me over!" Johnny attempted several more calls, with no success. As I was making my final corrections to land, I asked Johnny to take the controls, because, "This guy is probably going to ram us from behind." Johnny quickly took the controls, and made a right 45-degree turn to exit the runway. I knew that this Learjet was going to land right behind us, and I was going to see him out my left canopy any second passing us by, as he used up the remainder of the runway. The hair on the back of my neck was standing up.

I made a quick scan of a taxiway that crossed in front of us, using my Night Vision System, to make sure no traffic was in the way. I told Johnny, "It's clear in front." I used my right hand to grab the left side of the Optical Relay Tube (ORT) Fire Control Handles, to help me twist my body around to the left, to see out the canopy. I knew that I would see that Learjet passing right behind us, as we left the runway. At this point, I felt like I was in a dream. I found myself looking at the Fire Control Panel directly in front of my face, about 6 inches in front of me, to be more precise. I started wondering, "Why this is happening? Why am I bent over forward, and STARING at THIS panel?" I knew we were still flying, because I could feel us moving about in the air, as if in a hover. I felt like I was getting vertigo, which is a sensation of flying in one attitude but believing you're actually in a different attitude. I wasn't on the controls, so I told myself that I needed to stay away from them, until I figured out what was actually happening.

I took a long blink, and now I was holding the two Fire Control Handles, and my whole body was shaking back and forth, gently. There was no sound. I started to wonder how I drove home, and how I got into bed, next to my wife. I even thought about where I parked my Jeep. I took another long blink, and opened my eyes, and now I was shaking sideways, a little more violently than before; but I was still wondering, "How did I get home, and where did I park my Jeep?"

I took another long blink. As I opened my eyes again, my attention was grabbed by the Master Caution Warning Panel blinking in front of my face. What I saw illuminating was the "Low Rotor RPM" warning light. I remembered, from my training, that this was really not a good situation to be in; so, as loudly as I could, I voiced a warning to Johnny, and then I took another long blink.

I opened my eyes, and now felt my body shaking violently, sideways. I was now trying to convince myself that this was just a bad dream; and, any second now, my new wife of six months would wake me. I took another long blink, and my eyes were forced opened by what was now a severe, sideways shaking of my body. I was wondering what was happening, and if it would ever end. Up to that point, there was no sound, so I started thinking that it was a really bad nightmare, and surely my wife would feel my violent shaking and would wake me up.

Sound started to slowly come back, and I could hear something thumping the ground around me. As the noise grew louder, I began to realize, "Oh God, we're crashing!" The thumping sounds were the main rotor blades, impacting the ground all around the stricken aircraft.

As all of this was happening, I remembered several Vietnam era Cobra pilots telling me, "If you ever get in a crash in a Cobra, and if you have the presence of mind and the time to do it, make sure you duck your head down and to the left!" This is because, like the Apache, the front seat pilot normally gets his head cut off by the rotor blades flexing down and slicing through the front canopy.

I don't remember if I ducked my head or not; I just remember getting shaken so violently that the last thought going through my mind was, "Is this ever going to stop"? Then everything was quiet. I was still sitting in the cockpit, and I slowly opened my eyes and looked up through the canopy glass, which was cracked like a spider web. The stars were so bright and beautiful. They gave me a sense of peace, since they were the only thing that made sense at that moment.

I felt the cool night air gently blowing on my right side. I looked up and over to my right, and saw a dark figure standing there, looking down at me. He was talking to me, talking in that gibberish that sounded like Charlie Brown's teacher, "Wah-wah-whaa, wah-waah . . . ." All I could think was, "Who is this person talking to me, and what is he saying?" I closed my eyes. I then found myself in a "push-up" position, halfway out of the right-side canopy, with my hands in the warm, soft dirt. I saw a pair of feet, one on each side of my head, and all I could fathom was, "Oh, shit, I've been caught; now what do I do?"

Johnny took hold of me by the shoulders, and lifted me to my feet. I cried out in pain as he pulled on my right shoulder. I stood up and could see, in the distance, the lights to our hangars; but it was the shredded rotor blades of our helicopter which framed the lights that I took notice of. I asked Johnny, "What happened?" I heard the same response as before, that Charlie Brown gibberish that I couldn't understand. Then a wave of pain shot through my already trembling body.

Days later, Johnny told me that he had no clue how long we had been in the helicopter, and that it looked like no one was coming to rescue us.

We needed to walk back to the hangars, across the middle of the airport. Johnny was worried that I would collapse at any moment, due to possible internal injuries, and he was feeling nauseous. Neither of us felt we could cover the distance back to the hanger; but he also knew that, if he didn't keep me on my feet and himself going, there was no telling when we would be found. We made it the entire distance to the hangar before we were discovered by a mechanic who had driven his tractor towards us, thinking that our aircraft had broken down on the taxiway.

The Army's Accident Investigation Board concluded that the cause of the accident was "pilot error", although they never officially explained the sudden, un-commanded tail rotor inputs, or the two flight computer "black boxes" which failed. They also never openly disclosed "why" there had been a rash of similar episodes, of "un-commanded flight control inputs", throughout the entire Army's fleet of Apaches. Subsequently, all the inventories of the Apache Flight Computers were inspected for a known anomaly, and a certain software number, and were then replaced.

As for me, I had no clue as to what had happened. I could only put together bits and pieces of the crash sequence. It took me months to recover from my physical injuries and, as I would later find out, years to realize the psychological injuries I had sustained.

The aftermath of a faulty fly-by-wire systems hiccup.
$18 million gone in mere seconds.

Chapter 2

War Preparations

Lisa *I always had so much confidence in him as a pilot and I never thought anything bad would happen. After his crash though, things changed. Whenever the phone rang late at night, I immediately would think something had happened to him but I never tried to stop him from flying. I knew that flying is what he loved to do and I would never have wanted to take that away from him. All I would do is say a prayer and hope everything went well.*

At one o'clock in the morning we waved at the bus that was taking Daniel away from us as his journey to Afghanistan began. It was a surreal experience and it didn't really hit us that he was going to be gone, in a war zone, for a year. We spent that night in a hotel near the base before driving home the next morning. Over the next couple of days small things would come up and I realized fully that I couldn't call him. It took our daughter about a month to really notice he was gone because for her whole life he was always in and out. For her, it was like he was on another trip at first. Our son asked constantly, "Where is Dad right now? When will he call? When will we know he has made it there? When will we get an email?" I tried to go on with life as usual but during that first month family and friends were calling incessantly asking if we had heard from him and whenever anything came on the news I would get a ton more calls. It was a constant reminder that life as we knew it was no more.

I was the second born son of four children of Mexican immigrants and grew up in a middle-class neighborhood in Houston, Texas. My dad worked two jobs and my mom worked full time in order to provide for us. I was your typical kid that rode skateboards and BMX bicycles. I played Army in the backyard when I was young but I never dreamed that I would actually join the Army.

I started college without any idea of what I wanted to major in but I eventually earned my Associates degree in Design drafting. I then transferred to the University of Houston, still unsure of what I wanted to major in. All I knew was that I needed to continue my education.

One of the courses I took was an ROTC Survival course. The Instructor of the class was a Special Forces Sergeant First Class. One day I was setting up small snares for animals, in a local park, as part of the class when he came over and asked me what I wanted out of this class. I told him I really didn't know; the class sounded like fun and it was outdoors instead of in a classroom. He suggested to me that maybe I should look into the Army to gain some maturity and get the College Fund. This way, he said, that once I figured out what I wanted to do with myself, I would at least have the money to pursue it.

Right there, he planted the seed in my mind that would forever change my life. I started thinking of my friends whose parents were successful and the one thing they all had in common was they had all served in the military.

I spoke with my dad who was in the Army years before I was born and told him that I was probably going to join. He then had one of his friends from work, who had been a Special Forces soldier in Vietnam, come over to our house to talk to me. He told me what the Army was like and said, "If you're going to be in the Army, go infantry. That way you'll know what the real Army is about. Even though the Army has plenty of technical jobs, the sole purpose of the Army is centered on the Infantry".

The next semester, instead of re-enrolling in college, I joined the Army.

I went to Fort Benning, Georgia for basic training, followed by my job specific training, Infantryman. This was the Army's **Home of the Infantry**. It was a whole new world for me, and to tell you the truth, I kind of liked it.

I ended up doing so well that I became the Distinguished Honor graduate for two companies. I was then assigned to Fort Carson, Colorado where I would serve with the 4th Infantry Division.

Several years later, when my enlistment was up, I was approached by my company commander to reenlist. He asked me what I wanted to do with my military career should I elect to stay in.

I thought about this for a while. I enjoyed being an infantryman, shooting all sorts of weapons and blowing things up. I liked the fact that I was getting paid to be outdoors, especially in the mountains of Colorado.

I had been assigned to a Reconnaissance platoon which involved lots of hiking, with lots of weight on your back. I learned how to call in airstrikes and artillery strikes. One of the big lessons I learned was, what I saw and read on a map, was usually 10 times steeper, longer and harder to walk in the real world.

Another cold hard fact I learned was that what I had seen in the movies was nothing like the real Army. Carrying an M-16, with an M203 grenade launcher attached to it looked glamorous on the big screen. In actuality, a true combat load on my vest and in my rucksack, weighed more than 100 pounds. Whenever my sergeant would say "we just need to get over that hill", I knew it was easier said than done, with all that weight on my back. I cannot even imagine how our grandfathers fought in World War I and World War II carrying all that weight with people shooting at them.

I finally told my Captain that I was interested in flying. He called a friend of his who was a Captain in the helicopter squadron at Fort Carson. When I went to talk to him, he informed me that I would have to sign an eight-year contract, with no guarantee of ever actually flying. He told me that at this time, the Army had more pilots than they could use. That didn't sound too promising, so I decided to get off of active-duty and go back to school. Active-duty was fun, but when all is said and done, you were still under the Army's constant control, 24 hours a day.

I now had my college money and several years of maturity under my belt. I came home to Houston and was about to start college when a friend of mine told me about a flying program that the military would pay for. That sounded interesting to me so I enrolled in the program, and that's when I realized that I liked flying, and found it easy to learn and study for.

Coming off of active-duty, I had also enlisted in a National Guard Long Range Reconnaissance Patrol (LRRP) unit; the unit was affiliated with the Airborne Rangers. To get into Company G. 143rd INF. LRRP, I had to prove myself first. The unit was full of Special Forces, Rangers, Snipers, and Navy Seal's, that had also come off of active-duty. The unit had patterned its special Selection and Training program after the famed British SAS.

Selection and training (S&T) for company G. was hard, but only for those who really cared about staying in. At any point and time you could quit, no questions asked. Modeled after all the Special Forces units around the world, this was all voluntary and there were more than enough volunteers standing by to fill the ranks.

I ended up staying with them for three years. During those three years, I learned a lot about self discipline, self motivation, and I matured. Being a LRRP was even harder than the active-duty time I did. There was no

Sergeant, Lieutenant, or Captain that would push you to complete a task, or to do your best. It was all up to me to stay in shape, study, learn, remember and then utilize everything, one weekend a month. Out here in the real world, I had to work a job, go to school, and maintain my physical fitness with nobody pushing me, but myself. On active duty, the only thing I had to worry about was being on time for formations and chow.

One summer, while on a training mission with the British SAS, I started thinking about looking into another career. It was easily 100° outside and I had been in the field for two weeks, getting bit by ticks and chiggers. In the distance I could hear a helicopter flying and I started looking around trying to see what type of helicopter it was. Within a few minutes, an AH-1 Cobra helicopter came hovering between the trees about 20 feet above the ground. I grabbed my camera and started taking pictures of this cool looking helicopter.

The pilot of the Cobra saw me taking pictures of him and started hovering around me, allowing me to take pictures of him from different angles. After a few minutes of his little air show, the front seater made a gesture with both his arms wrapping around himself indicating to me that his air-conditioner was working very well. He then made that international sign of tipping his fist up and moving his head back, then pointing at his watch indicating to me that he was headed to the Officers Club, to have a cold one.

Right then, I knew my days in the Infantry were coming to an end.

It was during this time with company G. that I was also getting my private pilots license using the G.I. Bill. Still not knowing what I really wanted to do with my life, I decided, that if need be, I would go back on active duty to fly for one of the military branches.

As luck would have it, there was a new Army reserve unit forming north of Houston. A recruiter told me that currently the unit had AH-1 Cobra helicopters, but would eventually transition to the newest attack helicopter, the AH-64 Apache helicopter. Being given the opportunity to be able to go to Army flight school was enough. Going to flight school knowing that I would be flying a Cobra helicopter would be a dream come true. The chance of having a shot to fly the Apache helicopter was beyond what I could even think of.

But as before, I had to be accepted into the 7th Squadron 6th Cavalry Regiment, Conroe Texas. I had to have a face-to-face interview with the squadron commander, Lieutenant Colonel Poland.

I had already passed a flight board consisting of a Colonel, a Major, and a Chief Warrant Officer 4. That board consisted of numerous aviation questions and personal questions and only allowed me the chance of being accepted into a squadron that may or may not send me to flight school.

Lt. Col. Poland was a Vietnam war veteran and a Continental Airlines Captain. He had traditions steeped heavily in the United States Cavalry, which he served with in Vietnam. Now he was charged with starting, from scratch, the newest and only US Army Reserve Attack helicopter squadron, with the designation of Cavalry.

I was a little overwhelmed when I first stepped into his office. It was one of those offices with a huge heavy wooden table in the center that was easily 15 feet long and there were all sorts of war memorabilia and awards that had something to do with the United States Cavalry hung on the walls. I introduced myself in proper military form.

Lt. Col. Poland asked me why he should spend the money to send me to flight school, and why I wanted to fly his helicopters. As he was asking me these questions, he leaned back in his official leather chair, and placed his feet on the edge of the table. To my surprise, he was wearing black leather boots, with spurs. I knew I'd better have a good answer for him. As I started explaining to him my background and goals, he stopped me midsentence, as he was looking through my file, and asked me if I was with Company G 143rd infantry LRRP. I told him yes, that I had passed their rigorous Selection and Training, and had been a member of that unit for almost 3 years.

Lt. Col. Poland, then looked at me, and smiled. He said that he knew several Special Forces soldiers in that unit. He went on to say, that he knew how tough that unit was, and knew of several missions that they had done. He said the interview stopped right then and there, he had only one more question for me. Lt. Col. Poland looked me straight in the eye, and asked "Are you willing to pull the trigger, to kill the enemy, when the time comes?"

I had only one answer for him, "Absolutely".

===

I had to quit my job before I left for flight school because there was no way I could leave a full-time job for a year and a half and expect my employer to keep it open for me. I put my civilian flight training that I was taking at a local college on hold as well.

Before leaving for flight school I had attained a private pilot airplane license and had enough time to complete the academic portion for the instrument rating in airplanes. I had heard that the highest washout rate from flight school was in the instrument phase of training and I would learn later, this statement was very true.

I didn't have a steady girlfriend when I left for flight school, which in hindsight proved to be a smart choice. Warrant Officer Candidate School and flight school were demanding and needed my full attention. There were a few flight school students who were married in my class and several brought their wives with them to live off post.

March of 1990, I arrived at Fort Rucker and was in-processed and assigned to the "A" company of Warrant Officer Candidate School (WOCS). I checked in to the old World War II barracks that had signs of all the years of use and abuse that one would expect of a two story wooden building that was very old. Upon checking in, I was assigned to an upper bunk in an open bay area, along with the rest of the candidates. Other than the foyer entrance and the communal bathroom, the main portion of the building was an open bay area full of steel framed bunk beds and individual wall lockers. The floor was covered with old tiles that were made of asbestos. The only reason the asbestos floor tiles were still in place was because it was more expensive and hazardous to rip them out and properly dispose of them than it was to just keep applying wax and letting them be.

Officially WOCS did not start for a few more days, during which, more and more people showed up, checked in, and started introducing themselves and asking questions about what the first morning was going to be like. Warrant Officer Candidate School (WOCS) is not just for pilots. The U.S. Army has Warrant Officers for other special jobs, i.e. Special Forces, Military Intelligence, Law enforcement and several other posts that require someone more specialized than an enlisted soldier.

Most of the WOCS students had prior experience in the Army in some form or another. Some were from the active duty Army and some, such as me, were in the National Guard or Reserves. Others were straight civilians that were taking advantage of the "high school to flight school" program. The Army was still the only branch of service that would take a person straight from high school and allow them the opportunity to fly.

One student, who came in from Detroit, had just turned 19 and was asking all of us experienced Army guys what he should expect. I listened in as several guys told him about graduating and flying Blackhawks, Chinooks or Huey helicopters, but no one really ever told him about what to expect the first morning and everything after that. Everyone seemed to only look at the end and not what was involved to get there. There were plenty of hazards, obstacles, training, and tests to get over or through before a candidate was awarded his silver wings. Other than Special Forces training as a medic, Army flight school was the longest and most challenging school the Army had to offer.

The kid from Detroit was young and immature and he washed out within the first hour of the first morning. I felt sorry for him, at first, because I could see a lot of myself in him when I was his age. He was naïve at what life expected from him and what the real world was really like outside of high school and home. From the first moment he arrived he acted like flight school was a "given" to him. He never seemed to comprehend that he was going to have to work hard for those silver wings. It seemed to him that since he had been accepted to WOCS and flight school it was his entitlement to get his wings.

As for me, I was getting anxious about the first morning because several stories had circulated about how the TAC (training and counseling) officers (which were the Warrant Officer version of drill sergeants) would treat the candidates. Thankfully, having been through the Army's basic training and infantry school at fort Benning, and doing my active duty infantry tour in Colorado, I was still in fairly good shape. I had learned and matured a lot since serving in company G as a LRRP, but I still had vivid memories of basic training and S&T and how much of a physical and psychological shock they were.

Memories of drill sergeant's screaming in my face and untold amounts of push-ups, sit-ups, miles and miles of running and every other physical training exercise that could be demanded of us to weed out any potential weak candidates, came back in vivid detail. But what I feared most was the long runs every morning. I could still run like the wind, but questioned if I was going to be good enough.

Five years earlier, at Fort Benning, I had finished basic training and graduated as the Distinguished Honor Graduate by, among other accomplishments, finishing the final physical fitness test with over 100 push-ups and 100 sit-up's within two minutes, and then completing a two-mile run in less than 10 1/2 minutes. I also never had problems running at the high altitude while based in Colorado. I attributed my physical fitness and endurance to growing up riding skateboards and BMX bicycles everywhere I went.

I was always too small to play most of the full contact sports with my friends and peers in high school, so I made up for it by riding skateboards in empty swimming pools and drainage ditches and actually did well enough to get picked up on a citywide skateboard team for a local skateboard shop.

On the last day of freedom, a TAC officer came into our barracks and demonstrated how our clothing and wall lockers were to be maintained. He showed us how to roll our socks, fold our T-shirts, and even fold our underwear. Most people who had never been in the military before found it ridiculous that we had to iron our T-shirts and underwear, but what was really ridiculous was how tight and perfect our socks had to be rolled. Each sock had to be rolled into a perfect 4 inch wide cylinder. When rolled perfectly, one sock was 4 inches wide by 1 1/2 inches round. Each sock could easily be placed into a 1 1/2 inch round barrel and fired like a bullet. They were rock solid when done correctly.

In each one of our wall lockers only authorized military uniforms were allowed. The entire purpose of everyone's wall lockers and clothing being the exact same was to be our first lesson in becoming a military pilot and paying attention to detail.

Planning a flight, preflighting an aircraft, flying the mission, and everything else that encompassed flying a multimillion dollar aircraft safely and efficiently required absolute attention to detail in every little step, so if someone was sloppy or lazy by nature, then the TAC Officers would either train that out of them or they would be gone from the program. I would assume somebody that had OCD (obsessive compulsive disorder) would do well in this program. As for me, I just wanted to make it through, no matter what I had to do.

Lights out was at 2100 (9 PM). I don't know if anybody else slept that night, but I just laid there anxiously wondering when the lights were going to come on.

Six hours later, I watched the door to the bay area fly open, the lights come on and a bunch of screaming TAC officers stormed in to wake us up for the first day's events.

0300—Just like basic training five years earlier, at least five TAC officers in black T-shirts, black baseball caps, woodland camouflage pants, and highly polished black boots were screaming and yelling as they were pulling and throwing guys that were still asleep out of their beds. Having been through this before, I quickly jumped out of my bed put on my running shoes and ran out of the building, like everyone else.

Running out of the building, there were more TAC officers screaming at us as they guided us towards the sand pit out behind our barracks. The only lights on were the stadium style lights shining down on the sand pit. Being in southern Alabama this early in the morning, a ground fog had formed over the sand pit. We all quickly made a formation and tried to listen to at least one TAC officer, out of the many others that were screaming at us, and start doing push-ups, sit-ups or whatever we could make out from all the screaming that was going on.

From prior experience, I knew that I had to at least be doing some type of calisthenics, whether it was the right one or not because God forbid if one or more TAC officers caught you trying to take a breather. This chaos went on for at least 15 minutes as the slower candidates were still making their way to the sand pit. Once everyone was finally in the sand pit, the TAC officers called us to attention. This was a thirty second breather and I looked around and saw steam coming off of everyone's foreheads. The senior TAC officer stood in front of us and said he would be the only one to give commands from here on out.

For the next hour we did untold amounts of different types of exercises. As much as possible, we all tried to maintain uniformity in whatever exercise we were told to do. Whenever someone would fall behind or stop doing flutter-kicks, or whatever exercise, there would be at least three or four TAC officers screaming in their faces motivating them to keep up. If someone failed to continue exercising, then the TAC officers would intensify the screaming and ask them if they wanted to quit right then and there.

Unbelievably, guys took them up on the offer and fell out. I looked up and saw several guys I thought were in better shape than me being escorted off of the sand pit. Several were throwing up as they stumbled away. That's when I saw the kid from Detroit getting half dragged and half stumbling on his own as he was escorted by several TAC officers. He was crying and throwing up at the same time. I never saw him again.

After the first hour of constant, grueling exercise, we were told to form up on the street that ran between the barracks. As soon as we were formed up, off we went on our first run. I think we ran for about an hour or so but time didn't matter because nobody was allowed to have a watch. All I could think was "keep running".

15

Getting into flight school, was a dream come true, and I knew, if for some reason, I didn't make it, I could grow old knowing I gave it 100 percent. I knew no matter what, I was not getting washed out in the first morning of the first day.

Just like the sand pit, after about 30 minutes into the run, guys were falling out left and right. There was even a former Drill Sergeant that was built like a rock, who found out his weakness was running. I never saw him again. I had started at the back of the formation when the run began and every time someone fell out we all moved forward to fill in his spot. Soon, I found myself at the head of my column in the formation.

As we continued running up and down one of the several hills, the guy carrying the Guidon (the flag that identified our class) started falling back and yelled for someone to get it from him. God forbid that Guidon hit the ground. No one stepped up so he looked back at me and handed me the Guidon as he fell out of the formation. I grabbed it and stepped up to the front of the formation and kept running. I ended up being the Guidon bearer for my flight class for the majority of flight school.

Now that I was "volunteered" as the official Guidon bearer, there was no way I could, or was ever going to fall out of any run.

Warrant Officer Candidate School and basic ground school lasted until the beginning of August 1990. August 4, 1990 I took my first flight, in a UH-1 Huey helicopter.

Shortly thereafter, Iraq invaded their neighbor, Kuwait. From that point on, flight school had a more serious and definite meaning. Most of the flight instructors were Vietnam era combat pilots who stressed to us how important it was to learn the basics of flying a helicopter, in order to safely make it through combat. For the duration of my flight training, our instructors hammered into us that we were being taught lessons on flying in combat that they had learned during the Vietnam War.

The barracks that I and the other flight students were living in were located directly across the street from the famed 1/229th "Flying Tigers" Apache helicopter squadron. Some days, between classes, we would see families gathered outside the hangar, saying their goodbyes as their spouses and dads were leaving for Saudi Arabia. That was a sobering sight, watching kids and wives crying as they hugged their husbands, realizing that they were shipping off to war.

As luck would have it, Desert Storm ended one month before I graduated from flight school. Army Warrant officer and Flight School lasts just over a year. During that time, I learned the basics of helicopter flying, flying in clouds under instrument conditions, and most importantly, basic combat skills.

I started flight school flying the UH-1 Huey helicopter and then graduated at the top of my class, rated to fly the AH-1F Cobra attack helicopter.

After graduating from flight school in April 1991, I went home to Houston to start my career flying in the Army reserves. I had to find a full-time job, and go back to school to finish my civilian flight training in hopes of getting a job flying for the airlines.

While in school I found a part-time job as a test subject with NASA. The only reason I chose this job was for a chance at getting a flight in the vomit comet. The vomit comet was a specialized NASA jet that was used to simulate zero gravity flight. It was used to help train astronauts and to conduct experiments in a zero gravity environment for the space station. In the beginning, I was not selected to fly in the vomit comet, although I was offered other jobs which were directly related to the space station. The pay was not bad and I could make several hundred dollars for very little time, which gave me all the extra time I needed to complete my flight training.

The flight school I was enrolled in had direct ties to a major airline and the program offered a graduating student an opportunity to get a foot in the door with minimal amount of flight time.

I was working for NASA, studying and flying to get a job with the airlines, and flying Cobra attack helicopters in the Army reserves. I would say I was doing pretty well.

August of 1991, I was invited to a friend's high school reunion. Having been in the Army since 1985 I had missed both of my own high school's five and ten year reunions. I had nothing better to do, so I tagged along. The reunion was actually several reunions at the same time. My friend's high school did not have a specific graduating class reunion; it had a reunion for all the students that graduated from their high school, regardless of the year they graduated.

It was held at an SPJST hall. It was a building that was used for large gatherings such as this. Once inside, the entire venue was crowded to the walls. Since I never went to the high school I really didn't know that many people there. Walking around aimlessly, I ran into a girl, Lydia, who had graduated from my high school. We both recognized each other, and simultaneously asked, "What are you doing here?".

She explained to me that her husband had graduated from this high school and I told her that my friend had graduated from there as well. After talking with her for a few moments, I realized that her husband worked with several people that we both knew from our high school. A girl with dirty blonde hair and beautiful hazel eyes came walking up all giddy and happy as we were talking. Lydia knew her because she worked with her husband and introduced me. It was very loud in there with music and lots of people talking, so I didn't hear her name clearly. She introduced herself to me then turned right around and told Lydia she would talk to her later and left.

Well, one thing was for sure, she was cute and full of life. Looking back at this now, I know what people mean by love at first sight.

After she left, I looked right over at Lydia and asked her, "Who was that girl?"

Lydia immediately sensed that I was really interested. I asked, or should I say, told Lydia that she had to introduce me to her again. Once she came back around, Lydia formally introduced Lisa to me. This was definitely not my normal way of meeting girls. I was usually shy and a little afraid.

For whatever reason, I knew I wanted to get to know Lisa better. So, despite knowing I had no clue how to dance, I asked Lisa to dance with me. Out on the dance floor Lisa and I made small talk, simple questions about how we knew people and I asked her where she worked, and then Lisa asked me what I did for a living. Without missing a beat, nor thinking about what I was about to say, I blurted out that I was working part-time at NASA with projects dealing with the space station, in flight training to get a job with a major airline, and was an Army officer and aviator who flew Cobra attack helicopters.

Lisa gave a quick "Uh-Huh", and said that she saw some friends she wanted to talk to, turned around and walked away. So there I was standing on the dance floor with the love of my life, walking away. I couldn't figure it out at first and then I realized what I told her I did for a living.

How could I be so stupid? Realizing what I told her I did for a living, her leaving, suddenly made sense to me. What girl in their right mind would believe a guy that just said what I did? Thinking about what I just told her, I wouldn't believe it either. I didn't know what to do. I knew I had to find her, and at least explain in more detail, what I did, or lie and tell her I was just a normal guy that bagged groceries for a living. All I knew was that I needed to find her, and never let her go.

Lisa and I started dating after our first meeting.

December 1991 I was to report to Fort Rucker Alabama again to start the Aircraft Qualification Course (AQC) for the AH-64A Apache helicopter. Since Lisa and I had only been dating for a few months she took the news pretty hard. She had not been associated with me during all my prior military experience so she thought that I was leaving for good. The Apache AQC was 13 weeks long which in Lisa's mind that was an eternity.

I was absolutely ecstatic about the course and the aircraft. The Apache was still fairly new to the Army inventory and was the most sophisticated attack helicopter in the world. Since I had already flown the Cobra helicopter, I was looking forward to what the Apache had to offer. The first few weeks of the AQC were ground and simulator classes on all the systems in the Apache. It was safer and more economical to train someone with the systems in the simulator first and then fly the actual aircraft.

The Cobra and Apache were essentially the same when viewed at the basic level. Both fired rockets, bullets and anti-tank missiles. Both had only two pilots, and both were the only Army helicopters that had an actual air-conditioner built in. The gun on the Apache was much larger in caliber and the missile on the Apache was laser guided as opposed to the Vietnam era wire guided anti-tank missile on the Cobra, and the Apache had its own night vision system built into the aircraft as opposed to using night vision goggles.

In ground school we were shown all the safety systems built into the Apache that were learned from experience in the Cobra. The Apache helicopter was far more capable and safer than any other attack helicopter in the world.

Just like flying airplanes, I was so enthralled with finally flying the Apache that I had no problems wanting to study and learn everything I could about it.

Even the feared "Bag" portion of AQC was no problem for me. The "Bag" portion of the Apache AQC referred to the night vision system portion of the course. It involved placing the student pilot in the backseat and covering all the windows with black vinyl covers. This allowed the instructor to fly in the front seat in daylight, and forced the student to fly strictly using the night vision system, from the backseat. The instructor, not having his vision covered up, could ensure a safe training flight. Many students had problems flying the "Bag" but most made it through this portion of the course after 15 or so flight hours.

The first time I actually walked up to the Apache was awe inspiring. The actual aircraft was much larger than I ever imagined, and after flying it, I was even more impressed, that size did not affect it's maneuverability at all.

Once again I finished at the top of my class and returned home afterwards.

==

September 11, 2001, I was in the briefing room of my job with U.S. Customs. Like most everyone else in the United States, I watched the news as they showed the attacks on the World Trade Center and the Pentagon. I was in a peculiar situation; I was still in the Army reserves flying the Apache helicopter and protecting our borders flying for U.S. Customs. I didn't know if I would be called up for the military or be sent somewhere around the country with my civilian job.

Like everyone else in government service, I was placed on alert. But it wasn't until less than a month later when the news was showing video of U.S. Army Airborne Rangers making a night jump into Kandahar, that my coworker, a Navy attack pilot and Commander, looked at me and said, "We may have missed Desert Storm, but we're going to get a piece of this one".

He was correct.

It was four years later when I got the call that I was being activated to go to Afghanistan.

I was a little nervous thinking that maybe I was going to Iraq. Every day the news was showing how many American soldiers were dying in that war. So I did a little research and found that there had been less than 100 deaths, total, in Afghanistan since October 2001. Most of those deaths were accidental and very few were actually combat related. The only major news that had come out of Afghanistan was the death of Pat Tillman, a football player who enlisted after 9-11 and after multiple tours of duty was shot by friendly fire in the mountains of Afghanistan.

November 7th 2005 was the day I reported with my reserve unit to start the in processing and mobilization for my one year tour in the Afghanistan war. It was a whirlwind time filled with paperwork, vaccination shots, weapons qualifications, classes and briefings. The actual training I received was questionable though, to say the very least.

We Apache pilots had to do training on improvised explosive device (IED) detection, Close Combat Battle house clearing, and the most ridiculous training of all, Guard Post Operations and arresting people. For some reason, I thought as an Apache Instructor Pilot, I would be getting and giving classes on Close Air Support, Aerial shooting, and anything else that had to do with flying in combat. All of us were frustrated at having to do irrelevant training when we had so little time to get ready to go to war.

A funny thing throughout all of our training was we were continually being told we would be going to Iraq. It seemed that all the briefings, all the training, and anything else, including vaccinations, were all geared for the Iraqi theater of operations. We would continually have to correct whoever was giving us classes, vaccinations, and even indigenous people briefings, and tell them that we were going to Afghanistan and not Iraq. At first it was comical, but after several days of this, we all looked at our orders to confirm that we were in fact going to Afghanistan, and not Iraq. Being in the military for a number of years, I knew that what the army said, and what the Army did were two different things. I would not believe what the Army said, until all was said and done.

However, we received a very professional and thorough briefing by a professor from USC (University of Southern California) about Afghanistan and its rich history. I never realized that most educated Afghan's were fluent in three different languages. Pashto and Urdu were the predominant local languages, but English and Spanish were also spoken. Another fact that we were told, was that the people of Afghanistan were referred to as Afghan's, not Afghani's, which referred to their money.

The professor discussed the British and Soviets failed attempts at conquering the country, along with the history of Alexander the Great and Genghis Khan, and their exploits through that country. I was never really much into History, but now that I was to be a part of that history, I listened intently.

December 2005 we were allowed to take a two-week break from our mobilization process for Christmas and New Year's. That was one Christmas that I did not take for granted while I was home with my family.

It finally gave me a chance to relax a little from the chaotic hustle of the mobilization process. I was sitting at the dinner table, going over all the legal paperwork that needed to be in order, should the worst happen. I was crunching numbers, and looking up information on the Internet. I figured out exactly how much of a pay cut I was going to take on this deployment. I was trying to figure out how I was going to tell my wife that they would have to make some sacrifices to their way of life while I was gone. I had to express that we really could not afford to have anything major happen to our car, house or pets. The money situation was going to be too tight for any unexpected surprises, for the entire year.

I looked out the back patio doors and saw my daughter standing by the pond. I did so much number crunching and situation guessing, my head hurt. I got up and walked out the back door and stood by the step to the patio. My daughter just stood there watching the goldfish in our pond, not saying anything or giving any other indication that she knew I was standing 10 feet behind, watching her. I stood there for a minute wondering, what was she thinking? Did she fully comprehend what I was about to do for the next year? Being the firstborn, she had always been very mature for her age, and was making straight A's in school. All her teachers had nothing but praises for her schoolwork and how she interacted with both her friends and adults. So, I decided to get everything out in the open and see what she really thought about her dad going to war. I was thinking that maybe she wouldn't answer me or she would ask me a bunch of questions. Either way, I knew I would have to find out what was going on in her mind.

I took a deep breath and asked her, "Shelby, what do you think about me going to war?" Without missing a beat, she replied "Dad, I know you're going to be okay, you're the best at what you do, and God told me he will take care of you, so I'm not worried"

Her answer left me speechless. I stood there for what seemed like minutes wondering what to say next. She had caught me completely off guard. She continued saying that she had been praying about this and had been reassured that everything was going to be okay. Not wanting to mess things up, as I usually do, all I said was, "that's great".

It never ceased to amaze me how mature Shelby was. My son, Eric, on the other hand, was a typical seven-year-old boy. All he wanted to do was play. I sat him down in his room and discussed with him where I was going, what I was to do, and the different outcomes, if things didn't work out the way I wanted. Once he realized that I was not going to be around for a year, he took it pretty hard. For the next two weeks everywhere I went, he was right by my side. I could tell he was scared and uncertain about what was ahead.

It was now the end of February 2006. My wife, Lisa, brought the kids up to Fort Hood for a final farewell. The sky was bleak and gray and it was very cold. We sat in the gymnasium, awaiting the buses to take us to the airfield. I told her that I would be out of touch for hopefully no more than a week. I just needed to get settled in and locate a phone or internet service. I reassured her that it was not going to be like the movies. I would not be getting off of a military transport plane, while under fire, ducking and shooting with people dying all around me. I told her I would also be real busy with all the additional in country briefings, and anything else, before I was to ever fly in actual combat.

It's a funny thing when you finally realize that you may never see someone you love ever again. I tried not to think about it, but here it was, the last moments with the love of my life. I wanted to say something prophetic and memorable, but I couldn't think of anything. We both just sat there holding each other, watching Shelby and Eric play with the other kids whose parents were also waiting to leave. I don't know if I was thinking of anything in particular, I was just in the moment, wondering what the future was going to bring. I don't remember how long it took or what I was doing at the moment the call came in. We were told to say our last goodbyes and line up to board the buses.

Lisa and I quickly called Shelby and Eric over to us. We made our own little family group hug then bowed our heads and said a prayer. As we said "Amen", I kissed and hugged Lisa one last time, and then did the same with Shelby and Eric.

So that was it. I could only imagine how that scene played out thousands, if not millions of times before. All the wars before, and all the wars that will come, American soldiers would bid their families farewell, and pray to God, that they would have a happy reunion, sooner, rather than later.

We boarded the buses and headed to the Fort Hood, airport. Once there, we got in line, had our IDs checked, and then sat down.

Once everybody had taken a seat, a nice gentleman, in civilian clothes went up to the podium and started talking about our service to our country, and how much the American people thanked us for our sacrifice. He continued on with a bunch of statistics that I thought were very interesting. He said that out of several million Americans that were of military age there was only about 1% that were actually in the military. Then, out of that 1%, only about 1% were actually in Combat Arms jobs. Out of that small percentage, the chances of actually being in combat, was also about 1%. Then, out of that small percentage, it was shown that even less than 1% would actually engage the enemy, face-to-face. The cold hard facts of this war, was that most of the casualties were not due to actual face-to-face shooting, they were from accidents, IED's, a very lucky rocket attack, and self-inflicted gunshots. He went on to say that in Afghanistan, those statistics were more the norm, than in Iraq.

He was basically trying to ease everyone's fears of the unknown, and was basically just killing time while they made the last minute preparations on our aircraft before we could get on board.

Once again, we were called to stand up and get ready to go onboard the aircraft. At this time, the gentleman asked if he could say a prayer for all of us as he had just informed us that he was a preacher.

An interesting thing about this was he did not have to say a prayer for any of us. He was there in case someone wanted to talk to him individually before we boarded the plane. His prayer was not one of those rehearsed, dressed up, I'm on TV and need more money, prayers. I could tell he meant his prayer from the bottom of his soul. It was one of those prayers I always knew God had intended a prayer to be. He asked God to personally take care of everyone of us and bring all of us home safely.

When he was finished, the whole room said "Amen". He then informed us that there was a lady standing by the door known to all as the Hugging Lady. She made sure every last one of us got a hug from her before we boarded. She was a small lady that reminded me a lot of what Mother Teresa would have looked like.

We walked out onto the tarmac where another line had formed at the bottom of the stairs leading up to the aircraft. Standing at the bottom of the stairs was the governor of Idaho, whose National Guard Apache unit we were attached to. He shook each one of our hands as we stepped onto the staircase leading up to the DC-10.

We departed the Central Texas military base around 10 o'clock in the morning. Everyone settled in for what was to be a very long flight. I reclined my seat, pulled a pillow around my head, and slowly dozed off.

I awoke to the flight attendant telling us we were preparing to land at the Bangor, Maine airport. We were stopping there to top off the fuel tanks before making the long trip across the northern Atlantic.

As the plane came to a stop at the terminal a Major got on the PA system and told everyone that we had two hours before the flight was to leave again. He said that we were to remain in the Main terminal and added that no one was to drink any alcohol.

My first thought was we're barely 5 hours into this one year tour and the Army is already controlling every aspect of my life. We all lined up to get off the plane and as I exited the walkway, to my surprise, it looked like half the city of Bangor had come out to greet us. I shook hands and thanked all the elderly people that were lining both sides of the walkway. They offered each and every one of us a cell phone to call home and check in with our loved ones. I called my wife and told her I was in Bangor, Maine and all was well. After that, I did something I'd always wanted to try; I went to the local restaurant in the terminal and stood in line to buy a famed Lobster Roll. One of the promises I had made to myself was I was going to do everything I could to not eat an MRE (Meal Ready to Eat).

That Lobster Roll was as good as everyone had said it would be.

Two hours later, we loaded back into the airplane and began the rest of our trip to Afghanistan.

We stopped in Kyrgyzstan, for a few days, before boarding an Air Force C-17 transport for the final leg into Bagram. Kyrgyzstan was unbelievably cold. I couldn't even imagine what it was like to be in Siberia. The flight from Kyrgyzstan to Bagram took us over the far western tip of the Himalayan mountain range. Since it was February, the mountains were all covered in snow. It was interesting to look out the window, and know that China was just off to the east.

We landed at Bagram airfield in the middle the afternoon. As the ramp came down in the back of the C-17, the airplane filled with a cool dusty breeze, punctuated by the occasional fumes of jet fuel. We walked out onto the tarmac and went directly to a bus that took us to the terminal. Sure enough, there was no gunfire, there were no rockets impacting, it was just your typical busy airfield. Looking around though, the mountains of the Hindu Kush rose up dramatically. You could see snow on all of the mountain tops and even in the shaded areas around us.

So this was a war zone.

We spent the next week moving into our homes, getting our final in country briefings, and preparing our aircraft to start flying.

===

My first flight in a combat zone was now imminent. I was flying with one of our instructor pilots that showed up two weeks before the rest of us. We were going to do a local area orientation flight around the "Bagram Bowl". I called the tower and requested clearance to depart to the east.

I started pulling the collective up with my left hand. The first indication I had that this was not a normal flight was the position of the collective. The aircraft would normally be coming off the ground to a five foot stable hover at 75% power but we were still sitting firmly on the tarmac. I continued pulling up on the collective and the aircraft finally came to a hover at close to 85% torque.

I knew we would be using a lot of power since we were fully loaded with ammunition, and were at Bagram's 5000 foot altitude, but it was unreal seeing it with my own eyes. I slowly added more power and moved the cyclic forward to start my takeoff. We took off along the runway to the North. I moved the cyclic slightly to the right to start my turn to the east. The aircraft was sluggish and not as responsive as I was used to. I made a few S-turns just to get used to the aircraft since I hadn't flown it in over a month.

Right then, I knew it would take all of my flying skills to maneuver over 8 tons of fully loaded aircraft in combat. I could then see why we were told in the briefings that the two main killers of aircraft here in Afghanistan were weather and the terrain.

As we started climbing in altitude, I finally got my first look of the area surrounding Bagram airfield. I had been anxiously awaiting this first flight.

Bagram was literally in a bowl. All around were mountains rising to over 12,000 feet. Everything to the east of Bagram was a wasteland of dry, hard packed dirt. I could barely make out the buildings that had crumbled from over 30 years of war. The homes blended in to the ground, not only because they had been destroyed by war, but because they were made from the ground they were sitting on. Strewn about was the wreckage of Soviet tanks and artillery pieces that were destroyed by the Mujahedeen and American airpower. On the eastern edge of the airbase was a row of four vehicles that were chewing up the ground in perfect formation. They looked like the same kind of Combines you would find on any American farm. The difference in these vehicles, though, was that they were tearing up the ground in order to find land mines. All day long, for the previous two weeks, I would hear muffled explosions. Now I knew what they were. These mine clearing vehicles were doing the dangerous job of trying to clear this country of millions of landmines that the Soviets had planted.

A few miles further east of the airfield was our gunnery range, which was named East River Range. It was an area at the bottom of the mountains that bordered the East side of the Bagram bowl and it consisted of several Soviet tanks and remnants of other vehicles that I couldn't identify. I don't know who came up with the name East River Range, because there was no river to speak of in the area.

The first order of business was to make sure our aircraft were put back together correctly and could still shoot. We flew over the impact zone to make sure there were no Bedouins tending to their sheep in the area we were about to shoot. Once the impact zone was cleared, we called the Bagram airfield tower, which was the only radio controller in the area. The Bagram tower really didn't control the range; actually, nobody controlled the range. Whoever showed up first, and had the biggest gun at that time, owned the range.

I set up my first run which was to shoot the gun at an old Soviet tank. There wasn't much left of that tank because it had already been chewed apart by numerous other weapons. I lined up my sites, actioned the gun, and squeezed the trigger. The whole aircraft shook as a 10 round burst of 30 mm high explosive rounds fired. Each 30 mm shell is capable of penetrating over 4 inches of reinforced steel, and sending shrapnel killing anything within a 4 meter radius of the impact point. What was very interesting about those shells hitting that hulk was the lack of Hollywood style explosions and fire. For years, the only shells we shot were practice rounds that were simply a bullet, no explosives or anything else, just a bullet. This is the first time I had ever shot an actual combat load of High Explosive Dual-Purpose rounds. The difference in watching these rounds hit was the telltale sight of a dark gray cloud that emanated from each one. My first shot of 10 rounds all impacted on the tank. Now that the gun was sighted in I could fire some rockets to see if they needed any adjustments.

This was also the first time I shot a real combat load of High Explosive, Flechette, and White Phosphorous rockets. Just as before, I lined up my sights and fired several High Explosive rockets at the rusted hulk. Just like the bullets, the high explosive rockets exploding were anti-climatic. The only difference between the training rockets we fired and these was the dark gray cloud appearing where the rocket exploded, and the muffled thump that I could hear inside my cockpit. These rockets had 10 pounds worth of high explosive composition in their warheads and each one has a kill radius of 70 meters. Even though the dark gray cloud was only a few meters in diameter, anyone within the kill radius would be shredded by the explosive concussion, and the hot steel shrapnel flying through the air.

I then lined up to fire one of the Flechette rockets. Each Flechette rocket contained just less than 2000 hardened, 2 inch steel nails. They kill by piercing hardened steel or human flesh upon impact. Flechettes were first introduced to attack helicopters back in Vietnam. Instead of shooting one at a time, such as the High Explosive rockets, we would fire Flechette's in pairs. Firing two Flechette rockets, at the same time, would produce a wall of 2 inch steel nails, over 50 feet in diameter. Watching the Flechette rocket's firing through the air, about 800 meters in front of the aircraft, I saw the telltale red cloud which indicated the explosive charge had fired the contents of the rocket (the Flechette's). I then saw a perfect oval pattern on the dirt, as all the Flechette's impacted the ground. I thought that was pretty cool, and I sure wouldn't want that fired at me.

Finally, I lined up to fire a White Phosphorous (Willy "P") rocket. These rockets explode in a very prominent white cloud of a highly caustic, phosphorous chemical. These are mainly used to mark a target, so that others on the ground, or in the air, can easily locate and identify a specific area. The only problem with these rockets was that they were equipped with an older version rocket motor. This motor was vastly underpowered compared to the motors used on the other rockets. I pulled the trigger and instead of that solid, robust sounding swoosh of the other rockets, the swoosh made by this motor was weak. This rocket motor also had a much more pronounced smoke trail emanating from it. I could easily follow this rocket as it arced in front and impacted next to the rusted hulk. As this "Willy P" rocket exploded, a huge white cloud could be seen and it was definitely more of a Hollywood type explosion. The brilliant white cloud could easily be seen from miles away. I then saw why it was used to mark targets.

We continued our flight around the Bagram airbase landing on increasingly higher spots on the surrounding mountains. The Local Area Orientation (LAO) was designed to introduce you to a new airport and all the rules and procedures that are used to fly into it. We were also using this LAO to demonstrate to all the pilots the differences in handling characteristics of this aircraft at the different landing zones (LZ's).

Flying around to all the different landing zones was also a good history lesson. It seemed that each landing zone had a destroyed Soviet tank or artillery piece next to it, and judging by all the artillery pieces and their locations which looked down into the Bagram bowl, the Soviets held the high ground. The mountains surrounding Bagram were nothing but dirt and rock. There was actually no vegetation, whatsoever. As I landed at several of these LZ's, I couldn't help but wonder how that destroyed tank met its demise, and what happened to its crew?

After the LAO, the next order of business was an actual combat mission. The next day we were to shadow the Apache crew we were replacing that had already been there for the past year. We would be doing a "Ring Route". This was a mission that involved us following either a Blackhawk or a Chinook helicopter as they made the rounds to all the different Forward Operating Bases (FOB's) along the Afghan/Pakistan border. The Chinook's and Blackhawks would land at the FOB's and deliver ammunition, food, water, and replacement troops. We were to provide whatever firepower was needed to protect those helicopters.

We were attached to the 10th Mountain Division for this rotation, who did not have Apache's at their home base in Fort Drum, New York. We would find out later that the Aviation Battalion commander did not know how to fully utilize "The Apache's" that were assigned to him.

March 6th 2006, was the first day I flew in a real combat zone. The mission was a "Ring Route" that would take us east towards the city of Jalalabad, and then to the famed Khyber Pass. We would then head north along the border with Pakistan to FOB Asadabad. Then finish the day out by returning home to Bagram.

After getting the morning brief, I would go out to preflight my aircraft. As I would climb, crawl, open, and look at all the different parts of this aircraft, I would say a prayer. This would become my normal routine for the rest of the year. As I held or looked at a certain piece of the Apache that I was inspecting, I would ask God to make sure that part did not fail on this flight. Since it is a helicopter built by the lowest bidder, I thought it was kind of funny that I was saying a little prayer over each and every part. I didn't even realize that I was saying a prayer over the whole flight, each and every day for the entire year.

As we departed east away from the Bagram bowl, we crossed over a tremendous Canyon that would easily rival the Grand Canyon. We then entered the Tagab Valley. This is the Valley that the previous Apache crews had told us was unstable and could erupt with violence at any time. The captain we were replacing told us that they had only two shootings all year, and the Tagab Valley was the location for both. He said not to worry though, every where else is pretty quiet throughout the rest of the area of operation (AO). He also told us that since the Taliban was toppled in 2002, there was very little fighting going on in the northeast sector of Afghanistan. That was comforting news as I didn't mind the thought of spending the rest the year just admiring the mountains, rivers, and the history of Afghanistan.

We continued our flight east towards Jalalabad, and I noticed that all the roads were nothing but dirt paths that had been worn by whatever traffic was using it. The only paved road was the main highway, Route 1 that circled the country and one road that lead from Kabul to Jalalabad then on to the Khyber Pass. Other than the compounds, which were family homes, there were no modern looking buildings whatsoever. The only modern type buildings were the ones in Kabul, but most if not all were heavily damaged by the war. This was all desert and the only evidence of green was immediately alongside the few rivers that we crossed.

We flew just north of the city of Jalalabad as we made our way east towards the Khyber Pass. Jalalabad was a city that had paved roads and several buildings. It looked like the tallest building in the city was a central mosque with a typical round dome and a minaret sticking straight up. It was surrounded by, what I thought, was a parking lot. I found out later that the assumed parking lot was actually the area where people would kneel and pray. The mosque was also easily identified by the aqua blue dome that contrasted with the bland desert colored homes and buildings in the city surrounding it.

Continuing past Jalalabad, we followed the Kabul River. The river eventually turned north as we continued east, towards the town of Torkham. Torkham was the last town before entering the break in the mountains that was known as the Khyber Pass. It looks like any border town in the world. The buildings were all small, dilapidated shanties that bordered the Main Street. There was a long line of Jingle trucks, lined up, waiting to get through the security checkpoint.

This was the world famous Khyber Pass, and there I was circling it in an Apache helicopter. The two Chinook's we were escorting landed at a military outpost just outside the town of Torkham. I continued circling the outpost, and studying the pass.

15 minutes passed and both Chinook's departed the outpost and headed west then turned north along the Konar River Valley, towards FOB Asadabad. Flying along, the Konar River Valley, I noticed huge fields of brightly colored flowers. My wife appreciated beautiful flowers, so I took out my camera and started taking pictures. I was thinking she would love me sending her pictures of these fields with beautiful flowers, here in Afghanistan. As I finished taking my pictures, one of the other helicopters radioed back to us asking what we thought about all those heroin poppy fields we just flew over. I started busting out laughing. There I was taking

pictures of those beautiful fields, planted by those wonderful people in Afghanistan, that were growing flowers for who knows what, and then discovering that it was the main reason for this country's problems. My wife would get a kick out of that.

We landed at FOB Asadabad, unloaded the Chinook's, and refueled all the aircraft. We eventually flew back to Bagram, shut down, and filled out the paperwork for the day's flight.

That was my first combat flight. Nobody shot at us and in fact several people even waved at us. I got to fly amongst the famed Hindu Kush Mountains and saw the world famous Khyber Pass. Not a bad day at all. If the rest of the year, was going to be the same as this, other than being away from my family, this wasn't going to be so bad.

A few days later, I was given the next mission. My Lieutenant and I were to escort two Chinooks to the southeast region. We were to fly past the city of Kabul, then continue south towards Oruzgan-E (a.k.a. OE).

I was looking forward to that flight because we were going to fly right past another infamous location, the Shah-I-Khot Valley. The valley was made famous by being the location of a major battle in 2002, Operation Anaconda. The operation was a major offensive designed to trap and destroy a major element of the Taliban. The valley was also where a battle occurred on top of one of the overlooking mountain peaks named Takur Ghar that involved Special Forces, Army Rangers, a fallen Navy Seal, and a destroyed Chinook. I had read about this battle, and was excited that I would be flying through the same valley.

Flying past the city of Kabul, there were numerous destroyed Soviet tanks and artillery pieces lining the outskirts of the city. I really couldn't see the city itself, due to a thick smog layer that covered the entire area. The dark yellow smog was a shocking contrast to the white snow on the mountains surrounding the city. We continued south towards Gardez, which was just north of the Shah-I-Khot Valley. As we flew along the west side of the Shah-I-Khot Valley, I pulled out my video camera and started filming and taking pictures. I thought it was very cool to be flying over a valley that I had read about.

We continued south towards OE. A few miles south of the Shah-I—Khot Valley, we flew over a remote mountain village. I really couldn't see the village until I was almost on top of it; all the homes were made from the local dirt. These adobe homes blended in perfectly with the ground they were built on. They reminded me of adobe homes in southwest Colorado, at Mesa

Verde national Park. Our flight path took us directly over the center of the town at about 200 feet. The crowd below was a mixture of women running into their homes, hiding their faces with their veils, and children waving at us, as we flew over. Since I was taking pictures, my copilot the lieutenant, was at the controls of the aircraft. I waved back at the children that were waving at us. We continued on to OE, about 20 more miles ahead.

At OE, we refueled while the Chinook's unloaded their cargo of troops, mail, and ammunition. FOB OE was in the middle of the Valley on the outskirts of the city of Oruzgan. I looked down at my altimeter and saw that this FOB was over 8000 feet above sea level. I was amazed when I was told that over two thirds of the country was over 5000 feet above sea level. Everything around FOB OE, like most of the country, was desert. There was no vegetation to be seen anywhere and the only trees I had seen were within the compound walls.

Once the two Chinook's had finished their unloading and loading, they called me to say they were ready to take off. I came to a hover, as did the two Chinook's. Being 8000 feet above sea level, I was already at the top of my engine limits, trying to maintain a 5 foot hover. The two Chinook's that were in front of me started adding power, to make it over the walls of this FOB.

All of a sudden, I felt the full blast of wind coming off of the Chinook's rotors. The Rotor Wash nearly flipped me over as it slammed me back to the ground in a hail of rocks that were also being picked up and thrown around by their rotor wash. I quickly lowered the collective to the bottom. The entire aircraft was shaking due to the tremendous wind being generated by the two Chinook's taking off in front of me. Talk about an eye-opener! I sat on the FOB for another minute while I looked around at the canopy of my aircraft for any damage caused by the rocks that had just sprayed us. I asked the lieutenant, if he had any damage that he could see, he replied, "No".

The lieutenant, who was just out of flight school, asked me what had just happened. I told him that was a lesson learned. From then on, we had to do everything possible to stay away from the downwash generated by the Chinook helicopters.

We made a quick check of everything and departed the FOB. We made a beeline to catch up to the two Chinooks heading to the North.

As we approached the village that we had flown over an hour ago, one of the Chinooks called me on the radio. The lieutenant was at the controls of the aircraft while we were trying to catch up to them at 100 feet and 150 miles an hour. One of the Chinooks said that there was a suspicious looking individual pushing something on the trail they had just passed over. I looked out ahead, and sure enough, I could see two small dots on top of the ridgeline about a mile ahead of us. I told the lieutenant to slide right so we could look at what this was out the left side of the aircraft. As we approached the two small dots, I could see that one of the objects had stopped on the path.

The larger object continued to move away from the other one. Something didn't look right.

As we came closer, I could make out that the first object was an individual pushing a wheelbarrow and running as fast as he could. As we approached the scene, the lieutenant called out "I got them!"

I looked out the left window in an attempt to identify the objects when the lieutenant surprised me by rolling the aircraft hard left into an 80° banked turn.

At that same moment, I saw what was on the ground.

The first object, that was running, was a man pushing a wheelbarrow with a 4 or 5-year-old girl sitting on it. The second object, that had stopped, was a 6 or 7-year-old boy that was running in circles.

The lieutenant rolling the aircraft into that steep banked turn at the speed and altitude we were at caught me completely by surprise. The aircraft started dropping out of the sky like a rock. I immediately grabbed the controls and at the same time told him "I've got the controls!"

The aircraft started shuddering and shaking violently as we lost altitude. I was trying to regain control and level the aircraft so we could fly away from the ground and Afghans below us.

I could see the old man's face clearly. He was completely terrified at the helicopter that had made a hard turn, lots of noise, and was now less than 100 feet above him. I could see his teeth as he was screaming and running as fast as he could while pushing the home made wheelbarrow. I could see the little girl's face as she was hanging on for dear life, and shrieking, at all this noise, and her father running for his life. About 10 yards behind him the little boy was so terrified that all he could do was run in circles and scream at the top of his lungs.

I couldn't believe what the lieutenant had just done. I regained control of the aircraft and flew away from these poor Afghan civilians as fast as I could.

I wanted to somehow be able to fly back, land, and personally apologize for scaring them. I wish that, somehow, I had a "jettison Soccer ball with an apology letter" button that I could push and everything would be okay.

The face of the little boy and the terrified actions of him just running around in circles, going nowhere, reminded me of my son. I could not even imagine how that father felt as his daughter was screaming and he was trying to get away from this attack helicopter bearing down on them. I could only imagine what he had gone through before. Maybe he had seen someone he knew being attacked by the same type of Soviet helicopter, during the Soviet occupation.

Either way, the entire image was burned into my memory.

I called the two Chinook's and told them, "It was nothing. I'll catch up to you in a minute".

Once we were linked up with the other two Chinook's, I handed the controls back to the lieutenant. I wanted to scold him for what he had just done but I didn't know where to start. I was still thinking about those 3 civilians that we had just scared.

I finally settled down, cleared my mind, and began telling him what just happened. I began by telling him that we were no longer at sea level. The altitudes and the weights that we were flying at place us in a very precarious situation. We can't just go flying along and slamming this aircraft back and forth. We don't have the power to fly this aircraft as if we were back home or at sea level. I then told him that this country was still populated by innocent civilians. We can't go around thinking that we can just go shooting, or scaring the crap out of everybody we see. We don't need to be making any more enemies in the world.

Our Rules of Engagement (ROE) were still very loose when you actually think about it. We could literally shoot at anything we deemed "necessary". The ROE basically stated that we were to only shoot for self-defense or the defense of anyone who requested it. The ROE was not totally specific on much else. Out here in the open expanse of this war torn country a person could shoot someone and either not say anything or just explain that "that" person had shot first. No questions would have been asked. But being a God fearing Christian I knew the difference between what was right and what was wrong. I know that's what makes the difference between us as Americans, and other countries. Chances were, if you had a few too many "shootings" someone would eventually say something and an investigation would follow and if appropriate, justice would be swift. The rest of the flight back to Bagram was uneventful and quiet.

The gymnasium we waited at, on deployment morning

Chapter 3

Hindsight's Everything

Lisa   *It seemed like everything broke, including the children, right after he left. The car broke down, the lawnmower broke, the septic system went out, but these were minor things compared to having to take our daughter to the emergency room when she got off the school bus with her pants soaked in blood from a playground accident and taking our son to the doctor with a concussion after his own playground accident. There was no way to immediately contact Daniel and tell him his children were hurt. I could go through the Red Cross to contact him, but if he was on a mission, there was no way to get a hold of him. Then the dog was bitten by a snake and everyone was freaking out. We didn't really know what was wrong with him, but his face had swelled up. When we realized it was a snake, we all piled in the car to go to the emergency clinic. It was late at night so they had to keep him. He was fine, but $987 later I realized it was money we didn't have to spend. All of the small emergencies were magnified with Daniel's absence.*

The Pech River Valley runs west from the city of Asadabad towards Camp Blessing, which is situated about 15 miles west of the city. The river splits at that point with one branch going north up the Waygal Valley and the other branch going to the southwest, deeper into the Hindu Kush. Camp Blessing was no more than 5 miles from the Korengal outpost if you could go from point A to point B in a straight line. For us, there were several mountains that we had to fly around, so flying distance was about 10 miles. Sitting at the bottom of this Valley, the mountains rise from 2000 feet to well over 15,000 feet above sea level. This valley would be absolutely beautiful if it wasn't in the middle of a war zone.

So far most of the missions into the Konar river and Pech river valleys were during daylight hours. I rarely had to fly the midnight shift, which I did not mind doing. Most of my training before I was called up had been flying at night with the Apache's special night vision system. Night flying brought a different level of comfort for various reasons, particularly, the special dark paint job which made the Apache extremely difficult, if not impossible, to see at night without any special equipment. There were very few instances of an Apache getting hit by ground fire while flying at night. Since the first Gulf War, this is what the Apache was known for, flying in the darkest of nights and attacking by surprise.

So far, our maintenance guys had been doing a great job of keeping our aircraft flying 24/7 and this high level of maintenance was comforting. The thought of having to make an emergency landing due to a maintenance reason somewhere out there in Afghanistan was just a nightmare too scary to contemplate.

Working the night shift was tricky business here at Bagram airbase because it was so difficult to get sleep during the day. Like a small city, it was very busy and noisy during the daylight hours making sleep virtually impossible. To make matters worse, our "B" huts were located directly against the flight line. You had to sleep with earplugs in to keep out the noise of the busy airport located right outside your window.

The Army has three different types of huts in Bagram. "A" huts were steel shipping containers converted to "apartment" style complexes. "C" huts were standard issue U.S. Army circus style tents. Our "B" huts were wood buildings. The "B" hut was approximately 15x30 (ft) and we had eight men bunking in there. These buildings were Spartan at best. You could arrange your room anyway you wanted, as long as everyone agreed on the layout and it was safe. There were 2 air conditioning units for the entire hut that were located on each end of the hut, right above the entry/exit doors. These units were combination coolers and heaters and had a hard time keeping up with the elements they were required to operate in. In the summer the 100+ degree days would easily overwhelm them and in the winter it would be no surprise finding your water bottle frozen in your room in the morning. But this was still home and way better than having to live an entire year in a tent or worse yet, out in the open. If I ever thought these conditions were horrible all I had to do was either remember my days in the infantry or take a look at what our soldiers were living like out in the FOB's. No complaining here.

When we were assigned the night shift, I would secretly hope that I was not assigned to an escort mission that would last throughout the night. If there were no assigned missions then I could get on a special phone line and call my family during their daylight hours. But usually, whenever I made a call back to the states, I would get an answering machine. I had to keep reminding myself that even though I was fighting a war, life on my family's side of the world was going on as normal with a 12 hour time difference.

When I started the night shift I would get the normal briefing and then make my way out to the aircraft and complete my preflight. After I completed my preflight I would step out in front of my aircraft, where the few maintenance lights were not shining, and look up at the familiar, comforting glimmer of the stars. It always amazed me that they were the same stars my family would see 12 hours from then. I guess you could say I was still in shock at being on the other side of the world in an actual war zone. It was springtime and North up into the mountains, I could see thunderstorms that had built up during the day but were still lingering on into the night, with lightning shooting occasionally out of clouds.

Bagram airbase enforced light discipline, so it made seeing the stars up in the sky that much easier. Other than the smoke from several household fires in the surrounding area, there really wasn't that much air pollution. From the aircraft ramp, I could look out to the east at the East river gunnery range and see the tracers from some ground unit shooting at targets as they practiced or qualified with different weapons on the range. I pulled out my wallet and flashlight to look at a picture of my wife and children, and wondered what they were doing at that moment. I said a small prayer that nothing bad would happen that evening, walked back to the pilot's hooch, and found a cot to lie down on.

I dozed off for what seemed like several hours when I was awakened by Allen, my copilot for that evening. He said we needed to launch immediately. I grabbed my M4 and started heading out to my aircraft as he briefed me on where we were going. He told me that a ground convoy had been ambushed and was hit by an IED somewhere in the Pech river valley. It was relayed to us that there were several casualties and we needed to provide air cover until a ground rescue was mounted from Asadabad. We were also told that the A-10 Warthogs that were providing cover were running low on fuel and needed to return soon so we had to get on station overhead and provide cover for the stricken convoy.

Bill, our most senior instructor pilot in our troop, took the lead as we flew east away from Bagram. We took the usual route east over a mountain range and then across a large canyon towards Jalalabad. The flight was pretty quiet up until that point. About 20 miles west of Jalalabad, we cut the corner to the north, away from the city, to catch the Konar river north towards Asadabad. There was very little wind so the flight was fairly smooth. We were flying over a very desolate area at the foothills of the Hindu Kush. There were no lights, not even any Bedouin camp sites with their small campfires burning.

All was quiet and calm as the aircraft flew through the night. I was running through my mind what was to lie ahead once we reached the stricken convoy.

Then my "Master Warning" light came on indicating a possible major problem with my tail rotor. This light would come on occasionally during flight in turbulent conditions, but the air was silky smooth so I couldn't blame this warning on turbulence.

I called Bill and told him about my "master caution light and Vibe gearbox light" (vibration out of limits with one of our two tail rotor gear boxes) had come on. Bill never answered me. I didn't know if my radio call had actually gone out or what? Both lights were still on glaring at me, which meant that one of the gear boxes was having such a severe vibration that it alerted the master warning system to turn on the warning lights. The emergency procedure for those lights coming on, and staying on, was to land as soon as possible.

I called Bill again and he still did not respond. Both lights were on for what seemed like an eternity. In actuality, they were on for probably no more than about a minute. Bill still didn't respond to my radio calls, so Allen tried calling him but did not get through.

I mumbled under my breath, "this can't be happening, please God make this go away". As if on cue, both lights extinguished and never came back on again.

Neither Allen nor I said anything else.

We continued on up the Konar river valley towards Asadabad. As we neared FOB Asadabad, Bill made a radio call to find out the situation on the Pech river valley and the convoy that had been ambushed. FOB Asadabad told us that they were mounting a rescue convoy but it would still take a few hours to get to the site. We continued north a few more miles, past FOB Asadabad, then turned west into the Pech river valley. We had the coordinates of the ambush site and made a quick plan that Bill would stay west of the area and I would stay east of the area, so we could provide cover for the stricken convoy without getting in each other's way. As we neared the ambush site we called the convoy and ask them for a situation report.

The soldier on the other end of the radio was definitely shaken up. You could hear the fear choking up in his voice. Their commander had been killed in the IED attack, and two other soldiers were wounded. The soldier was very worried that they were about to get attacked again. We told him that we were in the area to provide cover for him and his convoy, and FOB Asadabad was mounting a ground convoy to come rescue them. He told us that the attack came from the north side of the valley, and that he had several soldiers on the north side of the road making sure that they were not surprised by another attack. He then called me and said that there were lights on the south side of the river and was afraid that they were flashlights from the Taliban about to attack him from the south side. I immediately started looking on the south side of the river with my night vision system in hopes of finding the Taliban and stopping another attack. I could see some lights underneath the low trees, near some homes. I asked the soldier if he could guide my flight path to the lights he was seeing. I would then drop some flares over that position to confirm what he was looking at.

I made several low passes over where the soldier guided me. Once I lined up my flight path to go over the suspected lights, I reached down with my thumb to manually fire off some flares.

I was startled at first by how bright the flares were and how low I was actually flying. The soldier immediately called on the radio telling me that's exactly where he saw the lights. I was getting ready to start shooting up the area in hopes of killing the people responsible for the convoy ambush. I could see several homes in that same spot. Allen and I were looking under the night vision system to make sure that when we started shooting we would not hit any innocent homes. I made several more passes even lower than before straining my vision to make sure we could actually see people with guns underneath the trees. I realized then that the winds had picked up in that valley and what we were seeing were campfires underneath the trees next to some homes. Apparently, the winds blowing through the trees made the campfires look like spotlights or flashlights moving underneath them.

I called the soldier back and told him what we discovered, to his relief. We continued circling his location for what seemed like an eternity. Since we were at the bottom of the valley amongst the mountains; we could not make a direct radio call to FOB Asadabad. We were starting to get anxious as to how much longer it would be before the convoy showed up.

Both Bill and I were looking at our fuel gauges and calculating, in our minds, how much time we had left to provide cover for the soldiers below. We came to the realization that we were running low on fuel and the rescue convoy was nowhere to be seen. I asked the soldier on the ground if he wanted me to fire some high explosive rockets on the north side of the valley to scare off any Taliban that may be preparing to mount another attack. He responded with a resounding yes! I told Bill what I was about to do and he said he would cover me and let me know if anyone started shooting at me. It is a very tight valley, especially at night, so I barely had enough room to maneuver. I flew on the south side of the valley, made my turn to the north. I lined up my sights, on my helmet mounted display, onto a ravine that worked its way from the road up to the top of the north side of the valley. My prior infantry training taught me that if it was me that was trying to sneak up on a convoy to plan an attack, I would follow this ravine as well.

I called the convoy soldier one more time to make sure his guys knew what I was about to do so no one would be surprised by the resulting explosions. I fired off two high explosive rockets, which I knew would wake up anybody in that valley that hadn't already been awakened by the sound of our Apache helicopters. I squeezed the trigger and that familiar and comforting loud swoosh echoed through my helmet and was followed by the site of two white hot rocket plumes streaking straight ahead and impacting with two bright explosions.

The convoy soldier called me on the radio to convey his relief at hearing those explosions coming from HIS air cover. As I got closer to the ravine that I had just fired at, I saw three houses very close to where my rockets impacted. There were no lights in those homes so I assumed they either didn't have electricity or they weren't occupied, but secretly, I was glad I didn't hit one of those homes by accident. I wouldn't want to hear later that I had killed some children or anyone else unintentionally.

We continued circling over the wounded convoy for about another hour. We then had to give them the bad news that we were running low on fuel and we would have to head back to FOB Asadabad, get some gas, and come back as soon as possible.

It was more than obvious that that soldier on the ground did not want us leaving. There were only three Humvee's and one of them was destroyed with the convoy commander dead inside. The soldier on the radio knew that once his Apache cover was gone he could possibly come under attack again. We reassured him that we would be back and that the ground convoy from Asadabad was on its way. Although, since we could not make any radio contact with FOB Asadabad, I really wasn't sure how far away help was for these soldiers in need on the ground below me.

I felt really bad leaving them but we were running very low on fuel. While flying back eastbound we saw the lights of the rescuers on the ground headed towards the wounded convoy. Though the rescue team was still at least 5 miles away, I felt confident that they could make it to the stricken convoy shortly. We landed at FOB Asadabad and re-fueled. While on the ground the base commander called to tell us to return to Bagram. He said that the rescue convoy was arriving at the wounded convoy and no longer needed our help. I asked if we could still fly back to them and provide cover as they made their way back to Asadabad. We were then told that the commander back at Bagram had called on the satellite communication radio (Satcom) and told us to return back to Bagram. With that information, we departed to the south, along the Konar river towards Jalalabad, then turned west across the lonely and dark desert towards Bagram. Both cockpits were very quiet on the flight back home. I was thinking about the ambushed convoy and how they must have felt on that lonely road, with their commander dead, and help not arriving for hours.

The landing back at the airbase was uneventful. It was close to three o'clock in the morning and most of the base was asleep. I was pretty happy because it was my last night on the midnight shift and I would now have the rest of the night to sleep before starting my shift the next day.

48 hours after the convoy had been ambushed; I was sitting in the briefing room, getting the day mission's weather and all of the other pertinent information. To my surprise, I was tasked, along with another Apache, to provide cover for a ground element that was going after a suspected IED bomb maker in the Pech river valley. There would be some Air Force A-10's overhead as well to help provide cover to the platoon that was to make the raid. There were three homes that were supposedly owned by the IED bomb maker. This person apparently was responsible for more than a few IED attacks and American fatalities that occurred on the main road in the Pech river valley.

Finally, I thought, we were to be proactive and go after a known enemy. This was one of those missions Apache pilots look forward to. We would be providing direct support to a ground element of infantry soldiers that were going after a known bad guy; a gun pilots dream.

We took off from Bagram close to five o'clock in the morning. It was still dark outside, but off to the east you could begin to see the glow of the rising sun. The faint outlines of the mountains were just visible.

It took us just under an hour to reach the location of the ground forces in the Pech river valley. They had already dismounted from their vehicles and were working their way up a ravine towards the three suspect homes.

From above, I could plainly see the three homes the soldiers were headed towards. They were the exact three homes that I almost shot with the rockets when I was providing security for that stricken convoy. If I had only known this piece of information that night, I definitely would've had no problem putting several high explosive rockets, followed up with some white phosphorous rockets into them just to liven things up a bit, and show we meant business.

I was circling over the ravine that the soldiers were walking in, when the A-10s overhead showed up, and called for us to give them a situation report. I let the lieutenant in the other Apache start coordinating with the A-10s to locate us. The sun was just barely lighting up the sky, so it was still very dark down in the ravine. I took off my forward looking infrared (Flir) that I was using to fly with and replaced it with the night vision goggles that were mounted on my helmet.

Flir does not see light, it only detects heat. Night vision goggles, on the other hand, detect visible light and amplify it over 5000 times. With the goggles on, I could see little flickers of light from each soldier's "Fireflies". The "Fireflies" are small, infrared lights that are only slightly larger than a 9 volt battery. American and special operations soldiers would wear these on their helmets because they are only visible using night vision goggles, so other friendly forces could identify them easily, but they are not visible to enemy eyes. The fireflies made it very easy for me to identify where all of our troops were.

The A-10s overhead had not found our two Apaches circling yet, since we were so far below them in the valley. Suddenly the radios came alive as Tusk 01, one of the A-10 pilots, called us to ask exactly where we were. While our lieutenant, in the other Apache, was still trying to describe the ravine and other physical attributes that would help the A-10s locate us, I fired off three flares manually. Over the radio, the A-10 pilot was asking questions, still trying to find us, when he abruptly stopped and said that he had seen my flares, and now had an exact location on me. Just like that, problem solved.

While we were circling overhead, I could tell the infantry guys were having a rough go at it. The terrain they were working in was brutal and hostile, and I could see them climbing and crawling over large boulders. The situation was made even worse by their heavy assault packs, which were full of ammunition and other combat necessities.

Watching these guys reminded me of my days as an infantry soldier with the 4th infantry division in Colorado Springs. I remembered trying to walk up, or better yet, climb steep rocky terrain that was well over a mile above sea level, with a 100 pound pack on my back. It was no easy task for me back then, and I could tell it was no easy task for these 10th Mountain division soldiers below me. They also had to deal with the possibility of the Taliban launching an attack on them at any moment. As I watched these brave men undertaking the difficult task, my resolve intensified. I was determined to do whatever was necessary to ensure their protection.

Thirty minutes went by and the soldiers reached the homes. They called on the radio to report that the houses were empty. Looking back, it was no surprise to hear that. It seemed like no matter how hard we tried, somebody would let the cat out of the bag, and the bad guys would get away. The good thing was, we had proof that these were the correct homes. Whoever had given us the intelligence about the suspected IED maker, and where he lived, was correct.

A problem with doing deliberate missions against an individual or a particular location was a lot depended on the quality and timeliness of the information we received from the locals. More often than not, it seemed the word would get out that we were looking for either a particular location, or a particular individual. Word would spread rapidly that the coalition forces were paying good hard cash for any information on some event that had just occurred, or about a person of interest.

Getting any information from a local would have to be vetted as quickly and quietly as possible. If the information was good, then we had to protect that individual and his family from revenge by the Taliban. Over the course of the year I had flown several escort missions to remote villages up in the mountains. We would have to relocate entire families away from their homes because the Taliban had brutally beaten the father. The family then had been threatened by the Taliban that they would come back to do more harm to the rest of the family, if they believed that they had helped the American forces.

On the other hand, we also had to protect ourselves from somebody giving us wrong or untimely information, just to get some money from the coalition forces. We also had to make sure that whatever information was given was also not a ploy to lure our soldiers into an ambush. That seemed to be the predominant problem here in the high country of Afghanistan. This area was extremely tribal. If the tribes liked you and defended you, then they defended you with their lives. This was very evident with operation "Redwing" that had occurred just one year prior.

When we first arrived at Bagram, we had to sit in on several secret Intel briefings. One of the briefings was the history and outcome of Operation Redwing. Several Special Forces Teams were sent out to different areas of the mountains west of the city of Asadabad to hunt down and kill a Taliban commander who had proved to be elusive, since he had the help of the local villages who would hide him. One of the teams had been compromised and all but one of them was killed. He was taken in by a local village and held safely until he was rescued by American soldiers. There was a little bit of comfort in knowing how that lone survivor had been helped by the local Afghans and eventually rescued by American forces.

The location that I was circling over was very near where Operation Redwing had occurred.

We contacted the ground commander and told him we were going to climb to the top of the mountain to check the top and back side to see if the bomb maker was hanging out, watching us from above.

A tired and out of breath voice came over the radio telling us that was a good idea and we should go ahead and do that.

We were about 1500 feet above sea level. The top of the mountain that the soldiers were climbing was close to 10,000 feet. I started pulling in as much power as I could without exceeding any limitations. I was hoping that maybe if I climbed fast enough, I could either surprise or catch the bomb maker before he could hide somewhere in a cave.

A little over a minute later, I had made it to the top of the mountain and was looking around with my naked eye now since the sun was already above the horizon to the east. I quickly called the A-10s to help us in our search to see if they could find anybody that may look suspicious up here in this rugged terrain. Tusk 01 said that since there was no action, they were headed north to see if anybody else had any action for them.

I didn't blame them for leaving. Looking at my air tasking order sheet, they were the only fixed wing attack assets in the air at the time. With the mountains being so high, they needed to make their rounds over different ridgelines to get in radio contact with somebody that might need their services.

I continued circling for a while longer in hopes of either flushing somebody out or having the ground guys call us on the radio for help.

We continued our circling and searching for another hour as the ground soldiers made their way back down the mountain to the main road. Once they were all accounted for, the commander gave me a go-ahead to return to FOB Asadabad, since they no longer needed us.

FOB Asadabad was less than a 10 minute flight from our present location, to the east. We did our usual, refueled then shut down the aircraft. We stepped into the tactical operations center (TOC) where we made secure communications with our headquarters back at Bagram airbase. We were told that there was going to be a flight of 2 Chinooks coming up from Jalalabad. We were to link up with them and escort them north to FOB Naray.

FOB Naray was the northernmost FOB in the Northeast sector of Afghanistan and I had only been up there once before. In that area the altitude of the mountains raises well into the upper teens and in some areas, the low 20's. This FOB was right on the Konar river like FOB Asadabad. Less than 2 miles away was Naray's eastern side of the valley, which was the Pakistan border. The main road running through the town of Naray was a major route from the northern tribal areas of Pakistan. The next major city to the north was Chitral, which is in Pakistan.

About an hour later, the two Chinooks finally showed up at FOB Asadabad. Allen and I made our way back out to our Apache and started it up. This mission seemed fairly easy. All we had to do was follow the two Chinooks up to Naray, drop off their cargo pick up anything else, and then return to Asadabad. It should take no more than an hour and a half total.

Once both Chinooks were ready to take off, I made sure to depart before them, to avoid damage from their tremendous rotor wash. The two Chinooks passed me on my left side as we flew over the actual city of Asadabad, 3 miles north of FOB Asadabad. I fell in trail behind them and noticed a fairly new open air compound that we were flying by. Routinely, I would look down into these compounds to see if there was anything interesting in them. In this particular compound, I saw about 20 or so school desks with kids sitting in them. All the kids looked up and waved at us as we flew by. I could easily see pencils and tablets and books on top of their desks, neatly stacked. Even the instructor was waving at us as we flew by. Seeing those children gave me a good feeling of accomplishment. Good things were finally starting to happen. I finally saw, with my own eyes, kids in a formalized school where all the supplies and desks had been supplied by the American government.

We continued north flying about 200 feet above the Konar river. Allen was on the controls and I was looking around at the river, the mountains, and the homes that people lived in.

The last time I flew up this valley, a different lieutenant was with me who was fairly new to flying. He had just finished flight school right before we were deployed. On that flight, I was doing the same thing, just looking around at the scenery. As I looked out the right side of the aircraft at some homes on the ground, there was a loud pop on my left canopy. I blurted out over the ICS, "We've been hit!", and then looked straight ahead to find a spot to land. I was startled because the lieutenant didn't say anything and we had been in-country no more than a month.

My first thought was that we had been hit by enemy gunfire. I quickly looked down at all the engine instruments to make sure we still had two good running engines. I also checked all the caution and warning lights to see if any were illuminated, but I still didn't know what that loud strike was. As I ran through all the emergency procedures I needed to complete to make an emergency landing out there, the lieutenant blurted out over the ICS "Relax, we just hit a bird". At first I thought he was joking because I didn't think a bird could make that loud of a pop hitting the aircraft, but then the lieutenant confessed that he had seen the bird coming at us, and decided not to try and avoid it. He said that it looked to him like it had smacked right on my canopy. When we returned from that mission, we found blood on my left canopy, and two huge dents on the engine intake on the left side. Talk about a wake-up call! Hearing a loud pop like that is definitely unnerving and a real eye-opener!

So as Allen and I flew up the Konar river, following the 2 Chinooks, I reminded myself to continuously glance forward to make sure we were not about to hit any wildlife flying around.

An interesting thing we saw on this flight was the guard towers, or Minarets, at the entrance to some of the valleys leading to the east into Pakistan. These Minarets were very old, and had an Asian castle type look to them. They were reminiscent of the days of Genghis Khan and Alexander the great. As we flew north along the Konar river valley, the mountains continued to rise higher and higher. The terrain was much like the San Juan Mountains in southwestern Colorado, very rocky with trees but no grass. Snow became more visible on the mountain tops surrounding us. The main road, following the river, was just a well worn dirt highway, with an occasional jingle truck bouncing along. The Konar River began to take on more of an iridescent blue color. I could tell it was flowing very fast by the size of the rapids and whirlpools along the way. I thought to myself, one day maybe I could take a family trip here and run the rapids in my kayak for fun. If it wasn't a war zone, that place could easily become an adventure tourist's Mecca. I had talked to a local Afghan at the bazaar in Jalalabad about starting up a river running trip up here in these mountains. I told him that he could easily make upwards of $200 per person per day guiding them through these beautiful rivers. And if he could arrange an overnight stay in a local family home, and eat local cuisine that would be even better. He replied, in perfect English, that I was correct but the Taliban would never allow that kind of access to foreigners in this country.

Once we arrived over FOB Naray, the Chinooks made their normal landing inside the wire of the FOB. Since this FOB was still fairly new and remote, they did not have fuel, nor did they have room for me to land while the Chinooks were being offloaded with supplies. So, I just circled around for close to 30 minutes and when I looked down at the activity around the Chinooks, I noticed they were not even close to being ready to leave. I called them on the radio and was informed they were having problems offloading some pallets and would be on the ground for at least another 30 minutes. I quickly calculated my remaining fuel and realized I would be cutting it very close to making it back to FOB Asadabad with enough fuel.

Finally, after another 45 minutes, they called that they were ready to depart and head south to FOB Asadabad. I had about 35 minutes of fuel left for the 20 minute flight and I was slightly relieved, but still concerned, because it was just cutting it too close for my comfort level. We never knew what was around the next corner in this country and in this war.

While we flew southbound, about 10 minutes north of FOB Asadabad, we got a call from a Special Forces group on the common air to ground frequency (CAG) wondering if we could offer them some help. I quickly got on the radio and responded to their call, asking specifically what they need for us to do. They said they wanted us to help them look for an insurgent at the foothills in front of them.

I checked my fuel status then called the Chinooks I was escorting and asked them if they wanted to circle the Konar river while I went about a mile west in a valley to help out the Special Forces guys. The air mission commander (AMC) of the lead Chinook said that they did not have the time to circle while I went hunting for some Taliban. I got back on the CAG with the SOF (Special Operations Forces) guy and told him that "unless he was in a life threatening situation, I could not help him at this time".

The SOF guy responded that it was not life-threatening and we could go on with our business.

We continued south to FOB Asadabad and the lead Chinook contacted the FOB controller and told them that we were five minutes north inbound to land. The controller said that the LZ was closed at that time because there was a fire mission going on. Knowing that I was going to be cutting it close on fuel anyway, I quickly asked the FOB controller if he knew how long the LZ would be closed. He responded with the usual answer in a war zone, "I don't know."

Since we could not circle directly over the city of Asadabad, the Chinooks turned back to the North, and started circling less than a mile from the previous request for support from the SOF guy.

Taking advantage of the situation I quickly called the SOF guy and told him that I could now help him with whatever he needed and that I could give him maybe five minutes of support before I had to leave due to low fuel.

I always made sure that I communicated to any ground unit or person to let them know that I was there for them. Five minutes may not have seemed like much time, but it was all I could give him and maybe that was all he needed.

Once I located the ground unit, the SOF guy told me that the ridgeline to his southwest is where a lone insurgent was hiding and taking potshots at them. He asked if I could fly over it and see if I could spot him.

From my viewpoint flying over the ridgeline, it was nothing more than a 30 second application of power with my left hand on the collective. To the soldiers on the ground it was a 30 minute hike up a steep, rock strewn hill with 60 pounds of combat gear on their backs, while somebody was possibly keeping you in their weapon site the whole time.

Being a former infantry soldier, I knew that everybody supported the infantry and here I was, 15 years after leaving the infantry job, supporting them from the air.

Watching my fuel level getting lower and lower, I circled the entire ridgeline as low as I dared for as long as I dared. A few minutes later I called back to the SOF guy and told him that I could not see anybody on the backside of that ridgeline. He told me "thanks" and that I was cleared to leave.

Being the consummate gun pilot, I asked him if he wouldn't mind if I just fired off several high explosive rockets into the ridgeline to maybe flush the insurgent out for them.

As expected, the SOF guy replied almost instantaneously with a "YES!" I quickly lined up my aircraft towards the ridgeline, "actioned up" my rockets and fired off 4 high explosive rockets along the ridgeline.

As the rockets lit off one by one, they impacted about 25 meters apart along the ridgeline. Simultaneously, the SOF soldier keyed up his radio and told me all the shots were exactly where he wanted and in the background I could hear my rockets exploding and echoing through the canyon.

Listening to the rockets actually exploding in the background, over the radio, sent chills up my spine. It gave me a brief glimpse of what I sounded like from the ground. I couldn't even imagine being the individual that was the recipient of my attack. Whether he knew it or not, I never saw him, and as far as I was concerned, I was just shooting up a ridgeline, not an actual person.

After this brief "show of force", I told the soldiers on the ground that I had to depart back to Asadabad because I was way low on gas.

I made the quick flight back to the Konar river valley and contacted the Chinook flight that was still circling. I asked the pilot in command of the lead Chinook if he had any word as to when we would be allowed back into the FOB. He replied that he still had not heard anything and he could still see the 155mm howitzer's shooting to the west.

The FOB Asadabad controller had rightfully closed down the landing zone because the howitzers were firing directly over it. For safety's sake, no aircraft operations were allowed while they were shooting the cannons.

I then called up to the FOB controller and asked him how much longer they expected the fire mission to continue? I also told him that I had maybe 10 minutes of fuel left before I would flameout both my engines. He replied that there is an ongoing fight In the Korengal valley, and he did not know how much longer they would continue shooting.

Again, I told him I was fuel critical in hopes that he would realize I wasn't joking around about my fuel state. He once again told me there was nothing he could do.

I told the Chinooks that I was going to work my way over to the FOB and see if I could sneak in under the guns. I figured if I was to flameout, at least I'll be right outside the wire of the FOB. I came in very low and very slow from the north to the actual FOB, which I knew was not safe. I was hoping that maybe the howitzer gunners might see me and get the hint that I needed to land but what I actually did, was sneak in at a hover underneath the direct line of fire from the big 155 guns shooting.

I figured I could defend my argument if somebody wanted to persecute me for landing without permission but it was either ditch an $18 million aircraft with two aviators in it, or get a butt chewing for disobeying an order.

Truthfully, I didn't think any of the rounds leaving the tubes would come all that close to my aircraft. What I was worried about more, was the concussion from the cannons firing, which could possibly have caused damage to my canopy or something else on the aircraft.

A week prior, a parked Chinook had all its windows broken out on one side when one of the howitzers fired off several volleys of high explosive rounds directly overhead, at less than 50 meters away.

As luck would have it, as soon as I touched down on the LZ, the fire mission was over, and the controller called for the other Chinooks to come in and land.

Upon landing, I glanced down at my fuel gauges to see how much fuel I had remaining. I sat there for a second, with a sense of frustration, knowing that I was within a few minutes of running completely out of gas.

After I refueled, a soldier came up to my canopy and told me how much gas they had given me. I did a quick calculation and figured I had less than 10 gallons of gas remaining in my tanks. It seemed that stretching out a mission to near fuel starvation was becoming more and more common. Back in America, I would've gotten reprimanded for landing with so little fuel on board. I never would've done this in peacetime.

After we were all refueled, we began our flight back to Bagram, to finish the day out.

Once again, I logged close to 12 hours sitting in the aircraft.

Looking out my left canopy, with a patch over a bullet hole from a previous mission. Asadabad and the Pech river valley are in the distance.

Alexander the Great guard tower in Konar river valley, at the mouth of a valley leading directly to Pakistan.

Pech river valley flying to the west.
IED site, that stranded SOF convoy several nights earlier,
is to the front about 2 miles on the right side of the valley.

Chapter 4

The Homecoming

Lisa   *The week before he came home for R&R was absolutely nuts. I didn't tell anyone but the kids right away that he was coming, because I knew he needed a real break and not constant activity. He needed down time. He emailed a friend mentioning he was coming and then the barrage of phone calls began. I let everyone know that he needed to see his family first. It needed to be low key, nothing big. After a while everyone got the idea and backed off. When he arrived home, we let him decide what he wanted to do. We tried to enjoy the time together without thinking about him leaving again. We put that thought to the backs of our minds. The second goodbye was much harder than the first. Now that I had talked to him, and knew what he was involved in over there, it was even worse to let him go back. Things had started to get back to normal a little bit, and we all started to feel like a family again . . . at home . . . together. Then he had to leave. I knew another couple whose husband didn't come home for his R&R because the wife knew she couldn't say goodbye to him again. Which is better? Not having to do the second goodbye or not having those two weeks together?*

I'd only been in country for four months. I'd been shot at several times, and shot back several times. I was looking forward to my upcoming return to the United States, for my mid tour break. It was amazing how fast time flew by. It seemed like I just got there and now it was time to go home for two weeks of rest and relaxation, or so I hoped.

By now we realized that the general support aviation brigade of the 10th Mountain division did not fully realize how to use the Apaches assigned to them. For the most part, all we'd been doing were escort missions for both Blackhawks and Chinooks on their daily ring routes to deliver food and insert troops to all the different outposts. Most everybody on the base, including myself, were still in shock at the loss of Colossal and all of its crew, not even a month before.

Colossal, a Chinook helicopter, was on a night mission to pick up ground soldiers 11,000 ft up in the mountains. There were 60 knot winds gusting up to 80 knots. They attempted a tailgate landing three times, which was landing only the aft part of the helicopter on the ground because they were on a ridgeline and there was no place large enough to land the entire helicopter. On the third attempt the aft rotor hit a tree, causing the helicopter to crash and killing everyone on board.

Tennessee National Guard also had a crash of one of their Apaches but both pilots survived.

Both accidents were just that, accidents. There was no hostile fire involved in either of the two crashes. When I looked at the pictures of Tennessee's destroyed Apache, it was hard to believe no one was killed in that crash and that, for the most part, both crewmembers were going to be okay. You could fit the remnants of that Apache in a 6x6 room. It was completely destroyed.

The crash of the Chinook was still weighing heavy on everybody in Bagram. I could not comprehend how an Apache crew could have allowed the crash to happen in the first place. I had several run-ins with our senior officer as to why he didn't say anything to try and prevent the crash. The greatest unanswered question for everyone on the base was why did the Apache leave the scene of the crash almost immediately after it happened? The ground troops for the 10th mountain division, who were on that mountain top, waiting to be picked up, had seen their friends die in that crash. They were especially angry at "those Apache guys" for leaving them on a mountaintop without any air cover.

The rest of us within Charlie Troop were doing as much damage control as possible with the 10th Mountain Chinook pilots. We still had 9 months left supporting them and if we did not resolve this as soon as possible, it was going to be a long lonely tour for all of us.

As time wore on, and the full story was finally known, only the two individuals that were involved with the crash of the Chinook were ostracized.

I continued my missions into the Korengal valley on a weekly if not daily basis.

Each mission into the Korengal was preceded by what we called, Suppression of Enemy Air Defense (SEAD). SEAD was an artillery action that came about from the Cold War and Vietnam. It comprised of firing salvos upon salvos of artillery shells into a known location and then having the attacking aircraft fly right over that location just as the last rounds finished exploding. This tactic would theoretically keep, if not destroy, the enemy air defense artillery from shooting down the incoming attacking aircraft. If the high explosive 8 inch artillery rounds didn't kill the enemy gun placements, then they would at least still be hunkered down not knowing when the artillery barrage would end. Timing is critical during a SEAD operation because you don't want to show up early and get caught flying over a location while artillery rounds are still falling. There is also the possibility that rounds could fall short. A SEAD operation is a great tool, but the consequences of one mistake could be catastrophic.

After the first month of resupply missions into the Korengal outpost, we started using the tactic of SEAD'ing the surrounding terrain in the Korengal valley right before we entered. It seemed this tactic worked very well for the aircraft landing on the KOP, but did very little to stop the enemy from shooting at us as we exited the valley to the north.

Every time I went into the Korengal valley, I stayed as close as possible to the KOP, circling overhead, for fear of getting hit by one of the artillery rounds they fired at the surrounding area. Meanwhile, the Chinook's or Blackhawks were on the ground below me. Occasionally, the two FOB's (camp Blessing, and FOB Asadabad) would fire artillery missions into the Eastern side of the Korengal Valley, close to the KOP, while we were there.

The 10th Mountain ground commander finally had enough of his troops getting shot at coming and going to the KOP from the North, the entrance of the valley.

During the morning's brief, we were told that the troop exchange mission into the KOP would be departing out of the Korengal valley to the south.

To a non-aviation person, this would make sense. If you are getting shot at coming and going from one direction, then change the direction. But, as in everything else, you have to know the whole story.

We were already halfway into May in Afghanistan and the days were starting to get hotter and hotter. The twin engine and twin rotor Chinook helicopters did not have too much of a performance problem in the hotter, thinner air of the mountains. It was the Blackhawks and the Apaches that would struggle, and it only got worse as the temperatures climbed.

On the day's mission, I was the only Apache escorting two Chinook's to drop off and pick up soldiers at the KOP. I looked over to the Chinook pilot in command and asked him why he wanted to do this? Why did he want to land at 6000 feet on the KOP, and then fly south and climb to 12,000 feet, all within 3 miles?

I told him that I would have some serious performance problems with my aircraft trying to keep up with him, much less trying to make it over the mountains in that short of a distance.

He replied to me, "This is what the 10th Mountain ground commander wants". I looked over to my copilot, the new lieutenant, and told him, "This is a really bad idea; we'll be sitting ducks trying to climb out of that Canyon in the middle of the day and trying to keep up and cover the Chinook's".

I even made it a point to go back and talk to the Chinook pilot in command (PIC) and let him know my concerns about trying this in the middle of the day. He agreed with me, but he said, "This is what the 10th Mountain ground commander wants, and that's what he was going to get". I was a little concerned when he also added, "That commander needs to see for himself how difficult it is to do certain things with these helicopters".

We were to make several runs into the KOP that day to fully exchange all the troops that were coming and going. We made our flight from Bagram to FOB Asadabad with no problem in about an hour. I didn't feel good about the mission from the start because it just didn't sound right, and I had a new lieutenant that I was still training.

This was the same lieutenant that almost crashed us into the ground by slamming the aircraft into a hard/steep banked turn over a father and his two kids.

On the first flight into the Korengal valley it was still fairly early in the morning, so the temperature was still rather cool. As I circled over the KOP, I watched as the Chinook on the ground had troops running onto an off of it rather quickly. Within a few short minutes the Chinook was ready and he called on the radio saying they were ready to depart to the south. I replied back with, "I'm about as ready as I'll ever be!"

He lifted off and applied maximum power as he headed south and climbed at the same time. I cheated a little bit, and was already circling and climbing over the KOP, so I already had a 500 foot advantage of altitude over the Chinook, but the Chinook was gaining speed and climbing really fast. I was doing everything I could to gain altitude, airspeed, and cover him, as we headed to the lowest portion of the ridgeline to the South.

As we climbed over 11,000 feet and approached the ridgeline that we would cross, I felt the need to at least shoot some rockets at the ridgeline. We would be crossing at less than 100 feet above the ground, which would be perfect range for any RPG's or small arms fire, if somebody happened to be in the forest under us. Since the weather was still cool, I was keeping up with the Chinook, but barely. I slid off to the left side of the Chinook since there was a rock wall to the right of us that went up even higher. I asked the Chinook pilot if he wouldn't mind me shooting some rockets ahead of us into the ridgeline we were approaching and about to cross.

Apparently, the Chinook was also having some performance issues with his whole cargo area now full of combat loaded troops. He replied with a resounding "yes!" So while still watching my engine instruments to make sure I didn't exceed any limitations, I slowly lined up my attack symbology onto the ridgeline about 800 meters in front of us. I then selected white phosphorous rockets for no specific reason whatsoever. I called back to the Chinook and told him to get ready because I was about to shoot off of his left side.

The Chinook pilot told me later, he called up his crew chiefs and told them to get ready to watch the Apache fire some rockets in front of them.

I fired off two rockets. There were simultaneous swooshes as the rockets fired off, one from each side of my aircraft.

I could smell the exhaust from the rockets, and to tell you the truth, I kind of liked that smell. It took only 3 to 4 seconds for both rockets to impact amongst the trees right at the top of the ridgeline in front of us.

It was mesmerizing, to watch them streak ahead and explode in a white cloud against the dark pine trees. There was a big white cloud in the middle and streaks of white phosphorous streaming out in all different directions. The Chinook pilot immediately got on the radio, and with a sense of glee in his voice said, "WOW! That was pretty cool watching those rockets you guys just shot!"

I also had a huge smile on my face from ear to ear! It wasn't often I got to shoot white phosphorous rockets, especially when nobody was shooting back!

I looked down at the tall pine trees, as we crested over the ridgeline barely 100 feet over the trees. Even with the two rocket shots in the area below us, there could still have been insurgents ready to shoot at us. We were low to the ground with very little forward airspeed as we crested over the ridgeline.

Our destination was a long descending valley that ended at the Konar river just south of Asadabad. We started our descent out of 12,000 feet down to the river valley, which was at 1000 feet. We had to lose altitude fast because we only had about 3 miles to lose 11,000 feet of altitude.

There are basically two ways you could lose all this altitude in a helicopter. One, you could lower the collective and maintain your speed as you descended, which was basically an autorotation. Using the autorotation method wasn't too bad, except you really had to watch your rotor RPMs at these altitudes, to make sure you didn't over speed the rotor system.

The next method, which I preferred, was to keep in as much power as possible, then push the nose over with the cyclic, and pick up as much speed as possible without exceeding any limitations. It was obvious the Chinook pilot was doing the same thing. He was dropping out of the sky like a rock, and picking up speed while he was doing it. I told my copilot "this is how it's done". Both the Chinook and I were racing down out of that valley at our maximum forward airspeed's for each of our aircraft, which was close to 200 knots.

It took about a minute to lose 11,000 feet of altitude. I don't know about the Chinook, but my vertical speed indicator was pegged out at well over 10,000 ft. /m rate of descent!

Once we reached the bottom of the Valley, we made a left turn, North up the Konar river valley for a few miles.

A few minutes later, we were in radio contact with FOB Asadabad telling them that we were inbound with the old troops, and were ready to pick up some more new troops to take back to the Korengal outpost.

At FOB Asadabad I landed behind the Chinook and a little bit off to the side, as a matter of habit. My before landing checks always included safe'ing my weapons, and making sure my flare system was also in the safe position. Knowing that the aircraft was built by the lowest bidder, I still didn't have full trust in all the electronics. The last thing I wanted to do was line up directly behind the Chinook, that was loading and unloading people, and have a rocket, somehow, find a way to shoot straight into the back of a fully loaded Chinook.

So I made it a habit to always land in front of the Chinook's or Blackhawks. If I couldn't do that, and I had to land directly behind them, then I would make sure to point the nose of my aircraft off to one side, and never directly at an aircraft in front of me. It was my old infantry training kicking in, always controlling the muzzle of your weapon's direction at all times.

I watched the last of the troops load up on to the Chinook. I departed the FOB before the Chinook could get in the air to avoid them throwing up rocks from their rotor system and avoiding the tremendous amount of rotor wash that came off of their blades.

The Chinook would keep an eye on me as I departed before him. Then I would let him pass off one of my sides and lead the flight back into the Korengal valley while I covered him from behind, this was Standard Operating Procedures (SOP).

Just like the previous time to the KOP, the Chinook landed and started unloading and loading troops simultaneously.

Camp Blessing, which was just west of the Korengal valley, started shooting 155MM rounds onto the eastern side of the Korengal valley, directly across the valley from the KOP. As before, I circled as close as I could over the top of the KOP to make sure I was not in the line of fire. The rounds were landing just east of the KOP, at about the same altitude I was circling. It was mesmerizing watching them impact the trees and the bare spots on the side of the mountain. Occasionally, we could hear the actual thumps of the rounds exploding.

My copilot and I discussed what would happen if one of those artillery rounds landed short and hit us. We both agreed it was a nonissue, because if a 155 round hit the aircraft in flight (or on the ground), death would be instantaneous, we would not feel a thing. It was a morbid, yet amusing conversation, as we circled and watched the huge explosions less than 800 meters away.

Once again the Chinook called and said he was ready to depart to the south again, and just like before, I told him I was ready.

We headed south towards the same saddle we crossed before since it was the lowest portion of the ridgeline we had to cross. I made a beeline for the rock wall that was on the right side. As we headed up to the ridgeline, I knew from prior experience, that the Sun's rays shining on the east facing wall would generate plenty of heat. If I could get close enough, I could possibly catch some thermals to help me climb over the ridgeline. Birds and Glider pilots use this phenomenon all the time to get altitude without using any engines.

So here we went again, climbing, pulling in maximum power and setting up for max rate of climb airspeed. Only this time, instead of being on the left of the Chinook as we climbed out, I was trying to get to the right side and slightly behind. That way I could be closer to the rock wall and hopefully catch some of the thermals.

I was at max power, with a fairly decent climb rate considering the heat of the day and a full combat load onboard. I wasn't feeling good about it though because my forward airspeed was barely over 80 knots. It felt like we were standing still.

The Apache, at 80 knots, basically has a level attitude instead of the nose being slightly dipped as in straight and level high speed forward flight. We were climbing up at about a 45° angle, with very little forward airspeed. This meant the aircraft itself was level if you were looking at it from the side.

Once again, I was really uncomfortable with the situation I was in. I was starting to fall slightly lower than the Chinook and was getting worried that I would end up in his downwash, depending which way the winds were coming. I also didn't want to get too close to the rock wall off my right side either because there were still trees, rocks and trails that could hide insurgents.

It was at this point I told my copilot, "See, this is what I was talking about. We have all the power available applied, and we are basically stuck where we're at. I have no room to maneuver. I can't lower the collective, nor can I apply any more power, and I can't pick up any more airspeed. We're sitting ducks".

The Chinook was about 300 meters in front of me, and slightly above my altitude and climbing. I was slightly to his right rear, about 100 meters from the rock wall on my right side, trying to catch whatever thermals I could get.

I could easily see the tail gunner sitting on the back ramp of the Chinook. As I was looking at him closely, I noticed what looked like smoke coming off of his aircraft.

I was about to call the Chinook and tell him that they might have something wrong with their aircraft. As I continued watching the tail gunner, I noticed some red streaks coming off of his gun. I then saw a puff of black smoke just left and below the Chinook. I sat there, for what seemed like forever, wondering what the smoke was, and what the red streaks were coming off of the back end of the Chinook.

I followed the red streaks to the right and that's when I saw them!

The tail gunner of the Chinook was shooting at a group of Taliban insurgents on the side of the mountain. Without even thinking, I actioned my gun, and was looking straight at the insurgents, as **they** realized there was an Apache less than 100 meters away and about to cross in front of them!

I could see about 10 insurgents with AK-47s as they were shooting at the Chinook. Their guns were still pointed at the Chinook as they all turned their heads toward me with a look of amazement. To them it must have seemed that I had come out of nowhere.

I literally could see the whites of their eyes, their scruffy beards, and their man dresses in full detail. It seemed to be in slow motion; as they all swung their guns around to start shooting at me. I simultaneously squeezed the trigger of my gun. I didn't even have enough time to tell my copilot I was shooting to the right, as my gun erupted with a 10 round burst of high explosive 30 mm rounds.

I saw my rounds impact amongst the insurgents, cutting several in half, all in a cloud of black high explosive dust. I saw the spent shells fly from their AK-47s, and the white flashes from their muzzles as they all shot point blank at me.

My first burst of 30 mm impacted more into the left half of the group. I quickly adjusted my aim to the right or behind the group and squeezed off a second 10 round burst of high explosive rounds. At the same time I saw a white flash and a cloud of dust erupt just to the left of the group. I could see the smoke trail of an RPG headed straight at my aircraft!

It felt as if time slowed down. I could see the football sized metallic object with a trail of gray smoke behind it as it tracked straight for my cockpit. It was as if the RPG was guided from the front of my aircraft to directly center mass. That insurgent knew exactly what he was doing, and he'd led my aircraft perfectly. The only thing the insurgent didn't calculate correctly was my climb rate. The RPG passed directly under my seat. I quickly glanced out the left side to see a black cloud burst, as the special airburst RPG exploded about 25 meters away.

I yelled out, "RPG left!", then quickly looked back to the right, with the gun still slaved to my helmet sight, and fired off another 10 round burst of 30 mm impacting again amongst the insurgents that were now clouded in smoke.

I squeezed the trigger again, to shoot another 10 round burst, but this time nothing happened. I squeezed the trigger again and again, and still nothing happened. I then looked at my symbology, superimposed over my right eye, and realized that my copilot had taken the gun away from me.

I was so focused on the shooting that I didn't remember hearing anything. It was then that sound came back to me. I could hear my copilot, as he was frantically moving his head left and right with the gun slaved to his helmet screaming out "Where? Where?"

That new flight lieutenant was going through a full-fledged "Helmet fire" In other words he was completely clueless and overwhelmed by information about what to do.

By this time we had crested over the ridgeline and were no longer within the insurgent's sights. My copilot was still clueless as to what had just transpired seconds before. The Chinook made a quick radio call saying that they had taken hits and had several wounded in back.

All I could think was, "shit!" I took the gun back away from my copilot and told him to settle down. The shooting was over.

I didn't know where to begin. I called back to the Chinook and told him I was still with him, and as far as I knew, I had not received any damage. I then shifted my frustration to my copilot and told him to never take the gun away from me, if he had no idea what I was shooting at or what he's shooting at, in the middle of a fight.

It was exactly what I thought would happen. Just because some ground commander wanted to do something his way, instead of listening to his experienced pilots, we now had a shot up Chinook and several wounded soldiers.

It never even entered my mind that the RPG was aimed by somebody who knew what they were doing. Whoever the insurgents were protecting was puzzling me. Both the Chinook and I seemed to have just stumbled upon a group of insurgents, that for some reason decided to attack us with a ferocity I had not seen as of yet.

This time, coming off the top of that mountain down to the Konar river valley, the Chinook and I went as fast as we dared.

We both landed at FOB Asadabad a few minutes later. As I was shutting down my aircraft, I saw the medics running to the back of the Chinook to carry wounded soldiers out. I couldn't believe what just happened. I felt bad because the Chinook I was charged to protect had been shot up right before my eyes.

The refueler's hooked up to my aircraft to add more gas and the armament personnel were refilling my gun and rockets.

After the soldiers finished topping off and rearming me, I shut down completely and jumped out. I quickly walked around and inspected all over my aircraft looking for bullet holes. I was sure I would have several bullet holes in my aircraft because there was no way any of those guys could have missed me at point blank range.

By the grace of God, there was no damage to be found anywhere on my aircraft. I stepped away from it and that's when it hit me. That RPG came real close to knocking me out of the sky. I walked to the Chinook and helped the crew and the pilots look for damage on their aircraft. Sure enough, there were quite a few bullet holes on the right side.

I then talked to the right waist gunner and the tail gunner of the Chinook to ask what they'd seen. Both of them agreed with me that as far as they knew, we had surprised some group of Taliban insurgents that were on the side of that mountain. They both said that the Taliban had opened fire on them first and they immediately returned fire. They also saw an RPG fired at them. The tail gunner said he saw the RPG fired at me pass within inches underneath my aircraft as it exploded several meters out my left side.

I then asked him, who was in his aircraft and who got hit? He replied that several Afghan National Army (ANA) soldiers were hit and wounded pretty bad. Then a crew chief who was standing on the aft rotor pylon, called down to tell us that they had been hit on one of the main rotor blades.

It had taken a direct hit right where the blade attached to the rotor hub. I climbed up there to take a closer look at the damage and the crew chief showed me the spot where the bullet impacted the blade cuff. The actual damage did not look all that bad, but apparently, the mechanics were afraid that there was spalling inside the blade that we could not see. I walked around the Chinook and found several more bullet holes all on the right side of the aircraft. I was still amazed and thankful that I had not taken any bullets at all. God was definitely looking out for me on that day. I still couldn't believe that all those insurgents had shot at me point blank, and none of them hit me. I said a prayer right then and there, thanking God that the RPG missed me. I had less than a week left before I went home to see my family again.

We remained at FOB Asadabad for about two hours while engineers back in the United States looked at pictures of the damaged blade, which were sent by satellite. We didn't know what we were going to do with the Chinook. Although it was safe within the confines of the FOB, sitting there for several days while mechanics fixed it would make a tempting target for the Taliban to possibly launch rockets at.

It was close to 4 o'clock in the afternoon local time when we got word that the Chinook was going to fly back to Bagram airbase on its own power. The only personnel that were going to fly on the aircraft were the minimum amount needed to safely conduct the flight; two pilots and three crew members in back.

We climbed back aboard our Apache and started the normal sequence to get ready to depart the FOB. Once the Chinook was up and running they called back to me to make sure that I was ready to go. I replied back with, "I'm following you and covering you, so you make the call, I'm ready to go!"

The second Chinook that was headed back with us was also ready to leave. As usual, I departed the FOB first, and made a right turn southbound for the flight home. Once southbound, I stayed to the eastside of the valley at minimum speed so the two Chinook's could catch up to me and take the lead.

I heard both Chinooks call that they were in the air, headed southbound, and had me in sight. I told them it was clear off my right side and that I was waiting for them to pass me by. Five minutes went by and I still had not seen either Chinook out my right window. Once again I called back to the Chinooks and asked them why they still hadn't passed me, since I was barely doing 40 knots.

Then it became obvious what the engineers had decided about the damaged rotor blade. Nobody had bothered to tell me what the engineers back in the United States had come up with for a temporary solution with the damaged blade.

The lead and damaged Chinook told me that the engineers, who had looked at the pictures via satellite, said they thought the aircraft would be safe to fly back to Bagram, as long as they stayed below 60 knots and less than 100 feet. To top it off, the engineers specifically told them that if something didn't feel or sound right, they were to land the aircraft immediately. I couldn't believe what I just heard, I wasn't comfortable with this plan at all.

Having that information would've been very helpful and I wished I had been told before we departed the FOB. The flight from Bagram to Asadabad normally took about an hour at 120 knots. We had to cross several extremely deep canyons, at least two ridgelines, and not to mention one valley that had an untold amount of insurgents in it.

The flight would now take over two and a half hours. The General Electric's I had on my aircraft burned over 500 pounds of fuel per hour per engine, minimum, just to stay running. At my combat weight I would burn twice that amount. This meant as long as the winds were favorable, I would be landing on fumes. If we ran into any headwinds or had to take a longer route to detour any hostile activity or locations, I would really be pushing my luck. I definitely did not want to run out of gas out here.

We were just cutting the corner out of the Konar river valley, northwest of Jalalabad. I calculated my fuel burn and status and made a quick call to the Chinooks to mention that maybe we should stop at Jalalabad before we continued so I could top off with fuel.

They both responded back that there was less than an hour and a half of daylight left and the flight had to be completed before it got dark.

So, we all continued westbound with me on a hope and a prayer that I would not run out of fuel. I kept thinking, "This is not how to complete a mission."

2 hours later, only the glow of the setting sun was visible to the west over the Hindu Kush Mountains. We'd crossed the last ridgeline before entering the Bagram bowl and as soon as we did, the radios came to life with the Bagram airfield tower giving final landing and takeoff clearances to different aircraft.

By this time my fuel gauge was down to the absolute very bottom of the LED indicator. I remembered reading in the operator's manual that the gauges are not reliable, two LED's ago. I finally told both Chinooks they were going to have to fly the last 15 miles unescorted because I needed to pull past them and at least get within the airfield confines, should my engines flameout.

I didn't think it was funny, but they both chuckled at my plan over the radio.

I called Bagram Tower and made my statement that "Deadwood was landing straight into bravo taxiway . . . minimum fuel". The phrase "minimum fuel" was international in the aviation world, meaning I could not screw around and needed to land ASAP. It might've been the tone of my voice or the way I said it, but the tower knew I was not joking around and they replied "cleared as requested" and nothing else.

I taxied straight to my parking spot and immediately started shutting down the engines, because now the only LEDs that were illuminated, was one red LED on my number one engine, and only the power is "ON" LED for my right engine. I had just made it with no time to spare.

The two Chinook's landed without incident, about 10 minutes later.

I jumped out of my aircraft and took off all my battle gear and body armor and let out a big sigh of relief and a thank you to God for getting me here without running out of gas. The fuel truck was already behind my aircraft and plugging into the fuel cell.

It was now totally dark. I couldn't believe I started the day's mission before the sun came up and finished it after the sun went down. The mission was supposed to have been over-with eight hours ago.

I made the long walk back to our command post, placed my M4 in the weapons locker and fell into the chair in front of the aircraft computer. As I was filling out the flight computer paperwork the crew chief came in and told me, in a matter-of-fact way, "Sir, did you know, they just refilled your aircraft with 465 gallons?" He then added, as if I didn't already know, "the aircraft only holds 475 gallons total, with the extra fuel tank!"

All I could do was shrug my shoulders, and say "yeah, yeah tell me something I don't know". I couldn't wait to start my out processing to go home for my R&R in less than a week.

The next week went by really fast. I only flew a few more missions, but was off the flight schedule for the most part, so that I could complete all the classes the Army required before I was allowed to take my vacation.

It seemed the Army was doing everything they could to educate soldiers about their upcoming meeting with their families, after being in a combat zone. There had been several incidences of soldiers having a difficult time reintegrating to civilian life after coming out of a war zone. It seemed some soldiers had either beaten their wives or gotten in trouble with the law during the few weeks that they were home on R&R.

As for me, I just wanted to get a decent night's sleep, in my own bed.

Before I knew it, I was on a C-17 headed to Kuwait. The only thing I have to say about Kuwait in June is . . . HOT! I have been to hot places before, but this place is absolutely, dangerously HOT!

Less than two days later I was on a charter flight headed back to the good ole USA. I don't remember too much of that flight, other than stopping off in Shannon Ireland, in the middle of the night, to stretch our legs and have the aircraft refueled and serviced for a few hours. But as soon as it was ready, there was no problem getting everybody back on the airplane and settled in for the final leg to Dallas-Fort Worth. It seemed as soon as the airplane lifted off the ground, everybody was fast asleep, including me.

About an hour before we were to land at DFW, the lights came on in the aircraft, and the flight attendants started waking everybody up. I slowly opened my eyes, and quickly looked around to make sure that I was indeed on a civilian aircraft headed home, and not in some kind of a dream. I opened up my window shade, and looked outside and saw a whole lot of green on the ground. I had to adjust my eyes to get used to the deep, dark, rich color of green after seeing nothing but light tan for the last six months.

Like everyone else, I started gathering my things from under the seat and around me in preparation for the arrival at DFW. I was straining my eyes and memory as I looked outside trying to figure out what part of the Dallas-Fort Worth area we were over. I soon realized we were landing to the south which was on the west end of the airport. It seemed rather surreal to look at the neighborhoods, the trees, and all the "normal activity" that was going on below. It was hard to comprehend that less than three days before I was flying an Apache helicopter in combat, on the other side of the world. As soon as the wheels on the plane touched the runway and we all felt that solid, reassuring deceleration, everyone gave a huge round of applause. We were all anxious to see Americans and normal stores where we could buy whatever we wanted.

I was also a little anxious looking at my connecting flight information, which would take me from Dallas to Houston.

The flight attendant told us the local time and date over the PA system. It was amazing how something as miniscule as knowing, or should I say, being told the local time and date was so important. I will never take that for granted again.

The plane exited the main runway and started taxiing towards the terminal building, looking out my window I saw some fire trucks driving down the taxiway and then I felt the plane make a left turn away from the terminal. I looked around and everybody else was mumbling and talking, wondering what the pilot was doing when we were so close to the terminal.

The captain came over the PA system to tell us the DFW fire Department was not quite ready to give us our welcome home "WASH". So now he was doing a quick 360 degree turn so that we would get our "mandatory" and official welcome home wash. I looked out the right side of the aircraft and saw the fire trucks pointed at us. The water nozzles came alive with a huge jet of water spraying over and on the aircraft. I never dreamed I would have a welcome like this.

Little did I know this was only the beginning.

The plane slowly approached the boarding gate and you could have heard a pin drop. As soon as the brakes were set and the "fasten seat belt" lights were turned off, there was another huge round of applause from everybody on board.

I closed my eyes and thanked God for getting me back to the good old United States safely.

We were off the plane and through the boarding gate, but the Army still had a hold on us. At the U.S. Customs location, we all got into formation so that we could be given some last-minute information. Some Army representative just said the basics about safety, and then we made a quick trip through the U.S. Customs lanes before we were released to get our baggage. He probably said some other things, but like everyone else in that formation, I was more concerned about getting my luggage, and making sure I did not miss my flight from DFW to Houston where I knew my wife and children were waiting for me.

After what seemed like an eternity, we made our way through the U.S. Customs lanes.

The person in the U.S. Customs booth asked the usual questions and then welcomed me home. Finally past the customs lines, there was a nice old man standing there pointing me in the direction of the escalators down to the baggage pickup. I was on a mission to pick up my baggage, make my way to my departure gate in time to board my flight, and finally see my family. To my surprise, the only people in the baggage pickup area were the soldiers that flew back with me on my flight. There was also another man, in a specially colored vest and hat with a clipboard, talking to several of the soldiers that had their luggage in their hands. I quickly found my baggage, and made my way to the man in the special vest, who asked me what my destination was. I very proudly told him Houston Texas. He looked down at his clipboard, said I was to be on the green shuttle bus and pointed me in the direction of the exit doors. I thanked him and made my way to the doors.

As I approached the opaque glass doors, they automatically swung open. To my surprise, standing on the other side of those doors, were the firefighters that were manning the fire trucks that had welcomed us home. They were lined up on both sides of the hallway in their uniforms, and they were all clapping and cheering, giving us high-fives and telling us "Thank you!"

One of the firefighters handed me a card. I quickly glanced down at it, and realized it was a picture of our aircraft as it was being washed by their fire hoses. On the back, every one of the firefighters had signed it with another, huge "thank you". I could hardly believe my eyes, as I was telling them, "Thank you, thank you", because I didn't know what else to say.

I made my way between all the firefighters and realized there was a female soldier walking beside me. I looked at her and she looked at me, and all I could say was, "Wow! That was awesome". Without hesitation, she replied back, "Boy, I'll say!"

We both continued a few more feet to a second set of opaque glass doors that had an exit sign printed on them. We approached the doors and they swung open automatically also. What I saw next completely took my breath away. As if those firefighters greeting us wasn't enough, what laid before me was a sight that every American needed to see.

There was a deafening round of cheering, applause, and clapping as several hundred men, women and children were lined up on both sides of the aisle. They were several people deep, waving American flags, handing out cookies, and telling me thank you and welcome home. I was left utterly speechless as I made my way between these people, wishing I could shake every hand and thank every one of them. I don't know if I even said anything. I put my hands out trying to personally thank each and every one. The procession seemed to last forever. The line went on and on. I felt tears well up in my eyes, and I had a huge smile on my face while I tried to mentally take a picture of the entire event so I could keep the moment alive. I wanted this to last forever.

I made it out of the last exit, where another gentleman asked me what color bus I needed. I know I must have said "Green" without even thinking because I don't remember saying anything. I was still in shock and awe from the greetings I had just received. The gentleman pointed me to a bus a few feet away. I don't even remember walking to the bus, but as I stepped onto the doorway, there was another American sitting in the driver's seat with a huge smile on his face welcoming me home.

He asked me, knowing what my response would be, "well, what did you think about that homecoming?" Once again, I don't even know if I said anything, because my face was frozen with a huge smile and tears in my eyes.

As I sat down, I looked over at the seat next to me and saw that same female soldier sitting there, with undoubtedly the same feelings as myself. Without even thinking, I asked her what she thought about that reception. She summed it up in one short sentence; "Wow, talk about emotional overload", with tears welling up in her eyes. I could not have agreed more.

The bus made a short drive to the terminal that my final flight left from. When I stepped off the bus, the driver once again thanked me from the bottom of his heart. I turned around, looked him in the eye, and told him "Thank you for your support and prayers"

I made my way to the terminal and checked in with the gate personnel of American Airlines. Since I was in uniform, she looked at me, recognized who I was and personally welcomed me home. She entered my reservation number in her computer to look up my flight status. I thought it was kind of funny looking at her, as she was tapping away on the computer and making different facial expressions, just like the ticket agent in the movie "Meet the Parents". She took my ticket, ripped it up in front of me, tossed it in the trash, and said "this isn't going to work". I really didn't care what she was going to do with the ticket, because at this point I could've walked from Dallas to Houston, and it wouldn't have mattered to me. She printed out a ticket and said "this is more fitting for you". She smiled at me, and said "here's your new ticket, your flight leaves in an hour". I looked down at my ticket and realized that she had placed me in the first row, in first class. I turned around, started walking, and finally started coming down from cloud nine after that unbelievable homecoming reception.

I made my way to the gate that my flight was to depart from and stood to the side to finally take a breather.

I looked around at all the people walking about. What really got me were all the different colors of clothing that people were wearing. It had only been six months, but obviously, seeing nothing but desert and high mountain scenery along with everyone dressed in digital camouflage, desensitized my eyes to all the different colors. It took a few minutes for me to adjust both my eyes and my thinking as to the normality of life that had been going on back here in the United States.

I was standing there in my uniform, minding my own business, looking around, when a lady came walking up to me. She was walking slowly, but

71

deliberately to where I was standing. I started preparing myself for what she may or may not say or do to me as she got closer.

She started up a conversation by asking me if I had just come back from Iraq. I told her no, that I was returning for my mid tour break from Afghanistan. She asked me what my rank was and what I did in the Army. I told her I was a Chief Warrant officer four and I fly the Apache helicopter. She smiled and said that her son was in Iraq, and that he always told her about how those Apache helicopters were really cool, and how everybody always looked to them to help them out whenever the enemy attacked. I smiled and said, "That's my job, I help out all those guys and girls on the ground, no matter what". I continued telling her how "it may seem cool to be flying over the landscape, but nothing gave me more pride and more satisfaction than to hear some soldier come up to me, days after we helped them, just to let me know how much they appreciated us helping them out. Or better yet to hear a soldier, tell me that if I hadn't been there when they needed me, they didn't know if they would've made it out alive". I continued to tell her how, "Nothing frustrated me more than to hear of one of our soldiers getting killed and thinking that maybe if I would've been there, I possibly could have done something to prevent that".

She quietly thanked me for my service and said she would pray for me, along with all the other soldiers in these two wars. I thanked her for her support and for her son's service in the military.

Time went by very quickly and before I knew it, I was boarding an American Airlines Super 80 headed for Houston. The flight was only going to last 45 minutes at the most. I sat down in first class and started thinking about how I would see my family, and what I would say when I saw them.

The plane came to a stop at the gate at Houston's George Bush international Airport. The flight attendant pointed at me and told me to come to the front by the exit door. The other first-class passengers behind me thanked me for my service and said I deserved to go first, so I could see my family soon as possible.

An hour earlier at the main terminal, TSA listened to my wife as she told them that her husband was on an American Airlines flight that would be arriving in less than 45 minutes. She asked them if there was anyway, she and our 7 and 11-year-old children could go to the actual arrival gate and meet their dad, who was coming back from the war in Afghanistan. The TSA supervisor pulled them aside into a special line and escorted them through security.

All three of them walked anxiously and nervously through the airport terminal to the arrival gate, and asked the gate attendant, if this was the gate that I would be coming in on. The American Airlines gate attendant confirmed what she was asking, and told them they could stand right there, in front, to wait for me to come out of the arrival walkway.

The flight attendant and the gate attendant opened up the door to the Super 80 aircraft, and they smiled at me, thanked me again for my service and said I was free to go up the walkway.

It was like seeing my wife for the first time over 17 years earlier. I had butterflies in my stomach and was secretly thinking, "I'd better not throw up". Out of my peripheral vision, I could see Shelby and Eric standing in front of her waving a sign. I don't even remember what that sign said. Lisa and I went straight to each other and hugged and kissed.

Apparently, we must of been there a long time, because I felt Shelby on one side and Eric on the other side tugging at my shirt saying "Daaaad!" Hearing that apparently opened up my ears, because that's when I realized there were people all around us in the terminal, clapping and cheering.

I now had 15 days to not worry about a war on the other side of the world.

. Or so I thought.

Mosque, south of Jalalabad near Tora Bora mountain range.

Shelby and Eric having me read their welcome home message
to them, at Bush International airport.

The slow flight back to Bagram, with the shot up Chinook from June 2006.
The sun was setting and we still had at least 45 minutes
to make it back to our airfield.

Chapter 5

Fight's On

Lisa   *When we found out he was being deployed to Afghanistan my first thought was I hated for him to be away from the kids for so long. I didn't think he would be killed but the thought of him missing out on the kids growing up if something did happen was my biggest fear. I knew there would be so much he would miss out on. He missed the kids winning awards at school, them performing in school programs, birthdays, anniversaries, Christmas. Special occasions would come up and I would get upset because the kids would get upset because all they wanted was their Dad to be there.*

The day started off on an incredibly high note. I guess I was still in shock at the reception in Dallas, and from finally seeing and holding my family.

I don't even remember getting my luggage, nor where our minivan was parked at the airport. Shelby and Eric walked very close to me on either side. I could see it in their eyes and their actions that they were not going to take their father being home for granted. I had to let Lisa drive, because I had not driven a vehicle, other than an attack helicopter, for well over six months. Riding in the passenger seat, instead of driving, was fine with me and I was actually anxious about all the traffic on the freeway flying by us. I'd been driving my entire life, but it was amazing how quickly I forgot how dangerous normal big-city traffic is. It's a war zone out there.

45 minutes later, as we pulled into my neighborhood, I was still trying to adjust my eyes to the immensity and richness of all the colors in the trees and surrounding vegetation. We pulled into our driveway and Shelby and Eric told my wife to stop the van so that I could see the sidewalk artwork that the neighborhood kids had drawn on our driveway. Shelby and Eric didn't want it ruined by driving over it, before I could get a good look at it. I hopped out of the minivan with my camera in hand and took pictures of the driveway artwork.

Even something as simple as reaching up and touching that automatic garage door opener was a treat. Shelby and Eric immediately opened the doors to the van and ordered me to stay in the garage until they could open the door of our house to make sure our dog, Cowboy, could give me his full welcome home lick-fest.

I walked into my home and saw the special banners that Shelby, Eric and Lisa had hung up to welcome me home. Familiar things, such as, the smell of the carpet, the kitchen, the dog, and the cat, was all I needed to finalize the fact that I was really home. If someone would've taken my blood pressure 10 minutes before, and then, the difference would've been dramatic. I could now relax and take it all in.

I literally didn't know what to do now that I was home. I tried to unpack what little luggage I had brought with me, but that did not sound all that appealing. I turned around and grabbed Lisa again and gave her another long kiss and a hug. We quietly said a thank you prayer for everything that we had.

The phone started ringing several minutes later. The first call was from my mom and dad, welcoming me home. Several other calls afterwards were from other family members, also welcoming me home. One call though, was from my two high school buddies who wanted to know if they could come over to see me in person. Without even thinking, I said "sure, come on over!" I then heard a loud throat clearing as I looked over and saw a surprised look on Lisa's face. That night we were supposed to have a quiet meal at home and watch a movie, which Lisa reminded me of in a hushed, frustrated tone. I tried to explain to her that my friends were leaving for a week, and I would not see them before I went back to Afghanistan. Being the good wife, she reluctantly agreed, but she put a one-hour time limit on their visit.

They showed up about an hour later. They started asking me questions like, what the war was like, and what the country was like. Without even thinking, I started telling them about the gun battle I had just gotten into a week prior. They both sat there listening intently as I was getting deeper and deeper into that day's events. I was telling them how that RPG almost hit me and all the gunfire that was happening that day. I didn't realize how detailed I was getting, telling them what had happened, until they stopped me midsentence and said that they had to leave. Once again, without even thinking, I told them they could stay longer. They both said they needed to leave as we walked outside into the garage. Once in the garage, away from my family, they told me that Lisa and the kids were sitting in the dining room, watching and listening to me tell my story. They said they could see a surprised and scared look on all three of their faces as I was describing their dad getting shot at in combat.

That was a wake-up call, telling me I needed to leave the war on the other side of the world, and be home, at least for the next 15 days.

After they left, Lisa, Shelby, Eric and I went back inside, and prepared the dinner table. When all was set and we were ready to eat, we all held hands and bowed our heads to pray. Shelby said her prayer out loud. She said the most heartfelt prayer I had ever heard, thanking God for everything we have, and especially for keeping all of us safe.

12 hours later, I jumped out of bed, looking around. I rubbed my eyes trying to focus on my new surroundings. I looked at my clock and tried to figure out if I was late for a mission brief or what? It slowly came back to me I was home and in my own bed. Everybody else was already awake, by at least three hours. I felt like I had just closed my eyes a few seconds ago. The long trip and jet lag, had taken its toll on me.

The next few days were spent fixing things around the house, and talking to friends and family that either called or came by to see me. Occasionally, I would sneak in to my office and check the Internet for any news coming out of Afghanistan. It still baffled me that there was so little information coming from there. The war in Iraq had total command of the media.

While surfing the Internet, I came across a news item stating that there had been a helicopter crash in Afghanistan. The news article only stated that the helicopter had a hard landing and there was one fatality. It did not specify what type of helicopter, or what area of the country the accident occurred.

Wanting and needing to know who was involved in that accident, I sent an e-mail to several people back at Bagram. I knew that all lines of communication would be stopped until the next of kin was notified first which could take several days. To my surprise, I received a response to my questions within a day. The accident happened three days prior, yet the media never reported the incident when it happened.

An Apache had crashed just outside of the Kandahar airbase. I was still not given the name of the pilot, nor which unit he was from. I would have to wait until I returned to find out all the details of the accident.

During the middle of my time home, we traveled to Lakeway near Austin, Texas, to spend the 4th of July at Lisa's brother's house. We went out on the boat and just enjoyed the water on beautiful Lake Travis.

That night, Lisa surprised me by making a dinner reservation for just the two of us, at a local Irish restaurant. This was different because normally the restaurant was not busy and didn't make anything special for their dinner selection. Lisa had told the owner about the occasion and he made sure that he had his best table ready along with a dessert that he normally didn't make. Knowing the circumstances surrounding our visit that night, the owner and his wife made us both feel more than welcomed and special.

Then Lisa surprised me again with reservations at a local resort hotel on the lake for the night. We had a bottle of Champaign and sat out on the deck watching the last of the fireworks displays all along the lake. Watching the fireworks and listening to the reports echoing over the water did remind me of the war, but they also reminded me of the true reason for the 4th of July holiday.

I looked over at Lisa gave her a kiss and then we clinked our glasses together and made a toast to everything we have and having the privilege of living in the greatest country in the world.

15 days went by faster than I ever expected. There I was, with my family, back at the airport. I had been on a whirlwind tour of Texas visiting family and friends and now, I was starting my long, lonely flight back to the other side of the world, to continue fighting the war.

Lisa, Shelby and Eric all had tears in their eyes as I turned around to walk onto the airplane.

Four days later, I couldn't remember any of the flight back to Afghanistan. I stepped off of the C-17 transport in Bagram and I felt like I never left.

The military had come up with a formula for determining how many hours of rest you need for every time zone you cross, to recover from any jet lag. So, instead of getting back into the aircraft and flying combat missions again, I went to several briefings to pass the time.

In one briefing, it was reported that the crash out of Kandahar was an accident. The Apache had launched on a quick reactionary force (QRF) mission at night. The flight was in response to a rocket attack at the Kandahar air base. Officially, no one knows why the Apache struck the ground. All I know is we lost a great man, a friend and a soldier. The second item in the briefing was of a combat medic that was killed. The cable winching up the medic and a mortally wounded soldier had broken, sending both of them to their deaths. As I found out more about that accident, I was furious.

Those two soldiers, and especially the combat medic, did not have to die that way.

Several days later I was assigned to my first mission since returning from R&R. It was standard operating procedure (SOP) for any pilot returning from R&R to fly their first mission with the senior instructor pilot. I totally agreed with the policy because going home on R&R and making the return trip, kept me out of the cockpit for just under a month. It only makes sense to fly with an experienced instructor before being sent out on your own, to get your mind back into the game, safely.

On my first mission I was to fly from the front seat of the Apache. Being an instructor, I was capable of flying and instructing from either seat. During my preflight, I was more anxious than normal, as I prepared to get into the front seat for the flight. The mission was to follow two Chinooks along the eastern border of Afghanistan, on a ring route. This meant we would be making several landings at FOB's situated along the Pakistani border.

Having several thousand hours in the Apache made preparing for this flight much easier. I climbed into the front seat and suddenly realized how small it was with my entire body armor and survival vest on. I thought this was a rather weird feeling, since I had done this same routine a thousand times before. I quickly forgot about those feelings and got into the same old rhythm.

We started up the aircraft, lined up behind the Chinook's, and departed to the south.

Flying south, away from Bagram, we passed just East of Kabul, then through a mountain pass across a vast barren desert, towards Gardez.

It was a clear day and the sky was a deep, dark blue. There were a few high cirrus clouds, which is a little unusual for Afghanistan. I think there are 360 days of absolutely clear skies every year. If you're not in the mountains, everything else in the country is barren desert. The only green patches of land are directly adjacent to any river.

I was at the controls as we followed behind the Chinooks we were providing cover for. I don't remember what I was thinking about because my mind was running on autopilot. Flying cover for any aircraft had become second nature.

I would fly level with the trail aircraft while looking ahead of them to their left and right. Then I would cross over to the left of the formation and check that area out by zigzagging back and forth behind the flight.

All while I tried to cover them from both sides, at the same time, as we flew to our intended destinations. At times I envisioned doing the same thing P-51 pilots did for their fellow aviators in B-17's during World War II.

Then out of nowhere it hit me. I felt a sudden wave of heat and nausea all at once. I started looking around left and right trying to figure out what was going on. I quickly reached down between my legs and adjusted the air conditioner vent to blow directly on my face. With my left hand I reached back over my left shoulder, and made sure that air conditioner vent was blowing down my neck. I was feeling tight all over, nauseous, and had a heat wave flowing over my entire body all at once. I felt like I was trapped inside a small box with my hands, feet and body tied down with no way for me to move. I didn't know what to say or do.

I told Bill, in the backseat, to take the flight controls. He told me he had the controls and asked me what was wrong. I quickly came up with a lie, telling him that I had a scratch on top of my head, and I needed to take my helmet off to get to it. Even before he said okay, I had taken off my helmet and could feel the heat coming off my head, like I had a fever. Sweat was pouring down my face. I adjusted both air conditioner vents to blow on my face and then started unzipping as much of my flight suit as I could reach, underneath my body armor and survival vest. I felt like I was going to lose my mind. I had to get out of the aircraft, right then. I didn't know what was going on. I started loosening up my safety harness as much as possible, thinking maybe that would help my situation. I was trying to think of some excuse to land the aircraft and get away from it. Either way, I had to get out right then.

And just like that, the feeling went away. I sat there, as we flew along, with my helmet in my hands wondering what just happened. I was soaking wet with my own sweat, and feeling a little chilled with the air conditioner blowing on my completely soaked flight suit. I put my helmet back on, zipped up my flight suit, and tightened up my seatbelt.

Bill asked me what happened. I didn't know what he had seen or heard, so I just told him I felt a hot spot in my helmet and needed to adjust it.

I don't even remember the rest of the day.

Later that night as I was lying in my room, I remembered what happened just before I went home on R&R. It seemed that I was starting to get claustrophobic for no reason. The last time I felt that way, was back in 1995.

Several months after my crash and I had recovered from my injuries, I was cleared to fly. Part of the post accident investigation was for me to fly in the same seat, and in the same conditions as when the accident happened. This was done with an instructor pilot so that he could go over any issues that may have caused the crash in the first place. I remembered getting in the front seat of the Apache for the first time after the crash. I remembered how tight and small the front seat was compared to before the accident.

This was all just psychological, because nothing physically changed in the cockpit. I quickly repressed those thoughts. I was young back then and still loved flying the aircraft. Basically, I just muscled my way through those feelings. Besides, real men don't fear anything, right?

Just after the last shoot out in the Korengal Valley, a week before I went home on R&R, I was sitting in the preparation briefings to go home. I remembered feeling anxious about being stuffed into a C-17 for hours on end. I actually had thoughts of canceling my R&R. I didn't want to get stuck in a crowded jet, for any length of time. I even made a visit to the 10th Mountain flight surgeon and asked him if there was something he could give me to alleviate my anxious, claustrophobic feelings. He said he could give me a pill, but never did. The only reason I didn't cancel my trip home, was the overpowering thoughts of being back with my family. The whirlwind shuffle of the entire process going home had preoccupied my mind.

The following day at the morning mission brief, I was told that we would be assigned to an actual "deliberate" operation. This was a surprise since the 10th Mountain division was very reluctant to use the Apaches for any planned combat missions. 10th Mountain seemed happy with us only flying armed escort for their Chinooks and Blackhawks. I could see where their train of thought was coming from. Special Forces were doing a good job of winning the hearts and minds of the Afghan people without much gunplay. If we could continue accomplishing our missions without any shooting it would be easier to deal with the Afghan tribal leaders. With the war going on in Iraq and other hot spots in the world, we didn't need to make any new enemies in Afghanistan by shooting any friendly's by accident.

The Air Force was already tied up with several friendly fire incidents in Iraq and Afghanistan. This was apparent whenever we would call the A-10s in to make a strafing run, or drop a bomb. The Air Force had strict protocol before they released any weapons, whenever any friendlies were in the area.

I'm sure it frustrated the Air Force pilots because it really frustrated the ground troops whenever they could not meet all the criteria to release weapons.

The mission encompassed Chinook helicopters inserting American Special Forces soldiers along with Afghan National Army soldiers (ANA), doing a "Snatch and Grab". In the Tagab Valley, 15 miles east of Bagram, Special Forces were going to capture a high-ranking anti-coalition commander that had been coordinating attacks in that area. The Special Operations Forces (SOF) guys would also look for weapons caches and any other information they might come upon.

The order of battle was for the Apaches to fly over the landing zone and make sure they were safe for the Chinooks to land on.

Since there were two Apaches on the mission we divided up the landing zone into two sections. I would take the northern section, and Sam (the pilot in command of the other Apache) would take the southern section. The Chinooks would land, the SOF guys would get out, and then the Chinooks would depart back to Bagram. We would continue circling the landing zone to provide any combat support for the SOF guys while they searched for the individuals and cleared several homes in the area. When the targets were captured and all the other tasks were completed, they would call back to Bagram and have the Chinooks come back and pick them up. We would all then fly back to Bagram and celebrate. If all went well, the entire mission would last no more than one hour.

A few hours later, we were sitting in the Apaches waiting on the taxiway at Bagram. The Chinooks were fully loaded with Special Forces combat troops. We started our departure eastbound to the Tagab Valley which would take about 15 minutes.

The lead Chinook was piloted by a highly competent female pilot, Mary. She was a no-nonsense aviator that everyone in her company respected. She was a hoot to talk to outside the aircraft, but when she was flying, it was all business. I had flown cover for her on several occasions and knew she could fly better than most of the male pilots in her company. It was kind of funny seeing her get in or out of her Chinook because of her size compared to the size of the huge transport helicopter. I had full confidence in her abilities to complete the mission, and I knew all those big tough Special Forces soldiers in the back of her Chinook did as well.

Two minutes before we crossed the last ridgeline into the Tagab Valley, Mary told us the code word over the radio that indicated for both Apaches to take the lead. I pulled in Max power as we dove off of the ridgeline leading into the Tagab Valley toward the landing zone. I looked ahead to confirm the LZ was directly off our nose. I dropped down to 50 feet at about 160 knots. Sam was at my five o'clock, and less than 100 meters away. As I came over the LZ, I banked left, and looked out at the ground and everything on my side, while Sam simultaneously banked right and looked at everything on his side. We checked with each other, over the radio, and agreed that the LZ was "ICE" (meaning cold, or no enemy in sight). I established my orbit, just north of the LZ, and Sam established his, just south. Both Chinooks showed up less than one minute later.

In the lead Chinook, Mary cleared the trees to the landing zone. Both Chinooks were "nose high" as they were slowing down to land. As she committed to landing to the forward half of the LZ, an individual was seen walking from right to left in front of the intended landing spot. She could not abort nor land short because of the Chinook behind her so she continued her landing. The individual, wearing his man-dress and baggy trousers, stopped in his tracks and watched as the Chinook came directly at him. Mary told me later there was nothing she could do so she landed on top of the guy. She called back to the rear of the aircraft and let them know that there was someone underneath the nose of her Chinook.

The rear cargo ramp of the Chinook was lowering down as the first Special Operations Forces (SOF) soldiers jumped out the back. The first group of SOF guys made their way to the front of the Chinook to see who was underneath the nose. The rest of the SOF and Afghan soldiers cleared out of the Chinooks and made their way to their intended targets. The first group reached underneath the front of the Chinook and pulled out the individual that was lying on the ground. He was completely stunned and had an AK-47 across his back. The SOF guys took away his weapon, then looked at his face and realized he was one of the individuals on the target list. They "flex cuffed" him, and stuffed him in the back of the Chinook, then told Mary to take this guy back to Bagram.

Circling overhead, we couldn't see much because of all the dust that the two Chinook's had kicked up. I watched nervously and prayed none of the Chinooks would lose sight of the other in the dust cloud and collide with each other. After what seemed like several minutes, I saw the first, and then the second Chinook emerge from out of the huge dust cloud. As they cleared the far end of the LZ, they made a left turn westbound, back to Bagram.

Following their script perfectly, the SOF teams started checking in on their radios. We could hear them perfectly as they said, all was clear, as they headed to the target houses. It took several minutes for the dust to finally clear out of the LZ.

Less than a minute later, the squelch broke on the radio, and we heard a garbled, weak transmission from one of the SOF teams on the ground. I called Sam and asked him if he heard the last transmission from the ground guys. Sam replied that he thought they said something about "taking fire". Sam tightened up his orbit and descended over one of the target houses to try and get better reception from the radio. I established myself on his right wing, and slightly higher, to cover him in case he came under fire.

We heard another garbled and weak transmission a few seconds later. This time, Sam said, "I think they said they were taking fire". We continued circling lower and closer, around the target house, hoping to either see what was going on, or maybe get a better understanding of what the SOF guys were trying to tell us.

I looked just below Sam's Apache at an orchard to his lower left, and something didn't seem right.

There was a 10 foot high dirt wall surrounding the orchard. From the orchard wall, there was another wall that bordered the eastern side of the LZ that the Chinooks had landed in. This wall extended south to another house about 200 meters away from the orchard. Something didn't look right between the orchard and the house to the south. As I looked at the house, I could see some of our Special Forces and Afghan soldiers climbing onto the roof, and begin pointing their weapons at the orchard 200 meters to the north. I looked at the house and it seemed as if the outer walls had dust coming off of them. I looked back north, at the wall to the orchard, and that same dust was on that wall. That's when I saw tracer fire coming from the house to the orchard and from the orchard to the house. The dust I was seeing was the dirt from the house and the wall coming apart, as bullets were hitting it.

Right then, Sam called me on the radio, and said they just got hit by gunfire from the orchard below him.

Fights on!

I could see Sam's 30 mm cannon blast away into the orchard, about 100 meters east of one of the other target houses. The radio from the SOF guys on the ground was blaring continuously, with intermittently intelligible words, saying that they were taking fire from the orchard. I could also make out some words that indicated one of the SOF teams was pinned down by machine gun fire from the orchard.

I was fairly certain that the enemy machine gun nest was in the orchard and our SOF team was across a 50 meter open area to the west, amongst trees and houses. I set myself up to make a rocket run coming from the west, over our SOF team. That way, as I dove in from the west, I would not fire any weapons until I was at least over our known friendly team's position. This would reduce the chance of me shooting short and having a friendly fire incident.

Since I was not completely certain about everyone's position, I decided I would only shoot one rocket into the orchard. Then I would ask the SOF team to adjust my fire from that impact point. My reasoning was if my shot was wrong, then only one rocket would impact, instead of several, thereby minimizing unwanted damage.

I was headed westbound and made sure I had all my switches set up to shoot only one high explosive rocket. I made a hard left turn while pulling up to gain altitude to set up a diving attack run.

Headed inbound to the east, toward the orchard, I lined up all of my attack symbology on my helmet display unit. I was going to squeeze the trigger only one time to make sure I fired only one rocket. I made one last check, lined up my symbology and squeezed the trigger once. At that same second, my "Master Warning" light came on, along with a tone in my helmet, which indicated my Stabilator was malfunctioning.

The aircraft pitched nose down and simultaneously one, two, three, (oh shit!) four and finally five rockets shot out of my rocket tubes. Something bad just happened. I pulled up out of my dive that had been exaggerated by the Stabilator, going full down, and driving the nose of my aircraft, steeper towards the ground. What happened? Only one rocket was supposed to shoot. All five rockets landed short, so much so, I couldn't even see where they hit below my aircraft. All the radios went silent, as I made a hard left turn. My copilot started shooting the gun at the ground to the left, while I made my turn. All I could think of was if I just hit our guys on the ground. What seemed like an eternity, which was only a few seconds later, the radios came back to life with a garbled transmission saying something like, "Good Shot!"

That was followed by my copilot saying, "Wow, all those rockets landed in that one spot, at the corner of the orchard. Good shooting".

Sometime during all that talk, I resumed my breathing, and my heart started beating again.

Sam and I traded shooting into that orchard for the next several minutes.

The radios finally came through a little clearer and we could understand everything the SOF guys were telling us from the ground. They told us to start checking the area around the three target houses for any more insurgents trying to make their way to the fight. I took the west side and Sam took the eastside of the LZ and started searching for anyone else that wanted a taste of this fight.

Just then, over the radio, Tusk 01, the lead pilot for a flight of two A-10s circling above us, checked in. He asked if there was anything he could do to help us out. Apparently, he had been watching us shoot up the orchard and wanted a piece of the action for himself. Sam's front seater started talking to Tusk. He told Tusk, that if they wanted to, they could make a gun run into the orchard. For the next several minutes Tusk asked us for all sorts of information on the orchard and about any friendly's that were in the area. The lieutenant spent the next several minutes talking between the SOF guys on the ground and the A-10s that wanted to make a gun run. Tusk 01 was trying to make sure that he had at least 150 meters of space between the target area and any friendly's to prevent any fratricide. When the lieutenant finally told him he had the required safety area between the intended impact point and any friendly's, Tusk 01 then asked for a 200 meter safety buffer between the impact zone and any friendly's. By this time, the Special Forces Sgt. on the ground (Beast 54), that was listening to this, told us, they no longer wanted any more shooting into the orchard. He said they were going into the orchard to look for any survivors.

I was disappointed at the news because I was hoping to be able to video the A-10s doing a gun run up close.

It was now close to an hour from when we started the mission. The two Chinooks were already cresting the ridge of the Tagab Valley, en route to the LZ. I was looking toward the LZ as I started seeing a red cloud of smoke coming up from the center of it. The SOF guys had thrown a red smoke grenade to mark the LZ and confirm the direction of the winds for the approaching helicopters.

Once again, the two Chinooks landed in a huge dust cloud. I couldn't help but worry that one of them would brownout and have an accident.

When the two Chinooks were on the ground, I could occasionally see some of the soldiers making their way from the tree line to the back of the Chinooks. It took no more than a minute for everyone to load up in the two helicopters to begin their flight back to Bagram. When the last Chinook departed to the west, I made a flight over the LZ, and banked over to see if anything was on the ground that may have been left behind.

I continued my flight west bound to catch up with the other Apache and the two Chinooks. Then the radio came alive with Tusk 01 saying that he was looking at the LZ, with his targeting pod, and saw something. We were now close to 5 miles away from the LZ when the next words he said sent chills up my spine. Tusk 01 said, "There's someone on the LZ".

All I could think was, oh God, we left someone behind!

I was about to call the Chinooks, and ask them to make sure their headcount was absolutely correct, when Tusk 01 said, "never mind, it looks like it's just a local scrounging around for spent shell casings."

I let out a huge sigh of relief, and started breathing again. The flight back to Bagram took less than 15 minutes.

After shutting down the aircraft, we all gathered around Sam's Apache. Apparently he wasn't kidding about taking a hit. Underneath the front seat was a hole that an armor piercing round had made. The mechanics looked at it and then started taking pictures. They then took off the panel that had the hole in it and out fell the bullet in one piece. We all took turns holding the bullet and admiring it as a cool war trophy.

I started walking across Steel Beach (the helicopter parking area) towards our command post, when I saw several individuals sitting on the ground. What caught my eye about these individuals was their clothing. They were all in native Afghan clothing. I also noticed the Special Forces guys standing around them, talking. The local Afghans on the ground had their hands handcuffed behind their backs, and goggles that were blacked out, over their eyes. That's when I realized they were the individuals that the SOF guys captured, less than an hour earlier.

I walked by and recognized some of the Special Forces guys that were in the briefing, and in the mission. I could tell they were busy, so all I did was wave, and tell them good job.

The next morning, the lieutenant and I went to go see the two A-10 drivers that were on the mission. I had made a DVD from my camera in hopes they would reciprocate with some gun footage of theirs we could have. Going to the Air Force side of Bagram airbase was interesting. The Air

Force definitely takes care of their own, even in a combat zone. You could tell that everything revolves around the pilots in the Air Force. The good thing for the lieutenant and me was we were in one piece flight suits, so every enlisted Air Force soldier that saw us, saluted us, and showed respect.

We finally caught up with one of the A-10 drivers that were on the mission in their planning room. We did the usual pilot thing and talked about each of our aircraft, and the mission we did the day before. I then showed them the DVD of the mission. The lieutenant put it into their player and it was kind of funny to see his response when he saw how low we were actually flying over the landscape. He blurted out "wow, so that's what those houses down there looked like". He said they rarely got below 5000 feet above ground level (AGL), so they never really got a "REAL" look at the homes and terrain that they fly over.

We asked him if he had made any videos of the mission. He said that they're targeting pod wasn't recording that day, and it wouldn't matter anyway because it records only in black-and-white and the detail isn't very good. He asked me what camera I used for my video because he had not seen any other video that was that detailed and clear. I told him it was just my own little camcorder that I was using to film as much as I could for my family back home. I also told him that our multi-thousand dollar digital recorder, in our multimillion dollar helicopter was normally useless also. We all laughed at the fact that here were two different, state-of-the-art aircraft, and each had a recorder, that didn't work.

We left the Air Force compound, and headed to the Chow Hall, for lunch. We found a place to sit near the back because it was nearly full. The food was not all that bad, and it was surely better than eating MRE's.

Several of us sat there enjoying our food, and tried to talk over everyone else that was talking in the Chow Hall. I glanced up at the main entrance of the Chow Hall and saw a staff sergeant standing in the doorway, looking around as if he was trying to find somebody. I could tell he was no ordinary sergeant; he was definitely in better shape than the average soldier. I thought, "Man, I wouldn't want him coming after me if he was looking for a fight". Just as I said that he pointed his finger straight at me. That's when I realized he was the Special Forces Staff Sergeant (Beast 54) that was on the mission the day before. He had cleaned himself up, and wasn't wearing his full battle rattle, which is why I didn't recognize him at first. I got up from my table and started walking to towards him as he was making a beeline straight for me. He shouted out, "You!", and I just responded with a loud, and nervous "Hey, You!"

We met pretty much in the middle the Chow Hall, shook hands and gave one of those brotherly hugs to each other. He had a huge smile on his face, as did I. He and I started exchanging thank you's while talking about the fight during the mission the day before. Staff Sergeant T (Beast 54) was one big tough Special Forces sergeant. You definitely wanted him on your side anywhere you went. But one thing was for sure, he was definitely a nice person. You just didn't want to be on his bad side.

I asked him about the radio communications after they had left the Chinook's, on the LZ (Landing Zone). He smiled and said, "Yeah, yeah, I know we had the wrong antenna on our radios. Those antennas worked fine, out in the open. But as soon as we got off of the LZ and underneath the trees, the antennas could not transmit through even a little bit of foliage." He went on to tell me that they started taking fire the second those Chinooks were gone, and the dust started clearing. He said they went to the first target house on the west side of the LZ and they were about to cross an alleyway, when their First Sergeant was hit by machine-gun fire that was in the corner of that orchard. The First Sergeant ended up on the other side of the alleyway from the rest of his team, wounded, and the rest of his team couldn't cross over to him because the machine gun was shooting straight down the alley. Every time they attempted to cross, the machine gun nest would lay down a wall of lead, which blocked their attempts at reaching the wounded First Sergeant.

He then added, "One of you Apaches knew exactly where that machine gun nest was. He flew directly over us and fired five high explosive rockets directly on it! That one volley of rockets knocked out that entire machine gun nest and when we went over to check out the damage afterwards, there were body parts lying everywhere."

I didn't want to tell him about the malfunction I had in my aircraft's flight controls and the five rockets shooting off, instead of one. I just smiled and told him "Yup, that was me, I meant to do that." While I said that, I tried to keep a straight face, thinking about what really happened.

He started talking about how much fun they had sitting behind the wall as our 30 mm shells were landing on top of them. He showed me pictures of them leaning up against the wall, smiling, and pointing up at us every time we flew over.

I asked him how their First Sergeant was doing. He said he was going to be fine. The lucky thing was the First Sergeant had just swapped his grenades from his left side to his right side. The bullet hit him just above his body armor, where his grenades would've been, if he had not swapped them over. The bullet hit his radio first and it took the brunt of the bullet, but it still penetrated his skin. It was not a life threatening wound just a wound he could talk about to his friends. There was no telling what would've happened if the First Sergeant's grenades would've been hit, instead of his radio.

We both stood there, in the middle of the Chow Hall, and discussed different things about that whole operation for several minutes. We paused for a moment, looked around, and realized that everyone in that small part of the Chow Hall had stopped talking and eating and were listening to our conversation about a battle that happened outside of their little world, Bagram. We both continued on with our conversation.

As I was talking to Staff Sgt. T., I noticed he was glancing at my "Coyote" troop patch on the right chest of my flight suit. I quickly reached up with my right hand and pulled the Velcro patch off of my flight suit and gave it to Staff Sgt. T. I told him that was the patch I was wearing during the mission yesterday. I didn't know what else to give him but that patch. Staff Sgt. T. reached over and pulled the "Long Tab" off of his right shoulder and proceeded to place the tabs and patch where my coyote patch was.

The "Long Tab" refers to the three tabs and one patch that identified a true Special Forces soldier. Beginning from the top, the first tab would be a Special Forces tab, followed underneath by a Ranger tab, followed underneath by an Airborne tab, with the Special Forces patch, underneath all of them.

All those tabs and the patch were indications that the person wearing them had volunteered at least four times, in defense of his country which was above and beyond the call of duty. He volunteered first to join the military, and then volunteered for Ranger school, Airborne school, and finally the toughest, longest school, out of all the military branches, Special Forces, in order to win the coveted Green Beret. Wearing those patches on his right shoulder also indicated that he had been in combat with the Special Forces.

Just about all the fights and combat support that I had been involved with in Afghanistan, involved US Army Special Forces.

It was with great pride that I wore, Staff Sgt. T.'s patches on my flight suit, where my "Coyote" troop patch had been.

I eventually took some of the video that I had from my cockpit, combined it with the pictures that Staff Sgt. T. had supplied, mixed it up with some music and gave it to him.

The meeting with Staff Sgt. T., and his thanks for helping them out during the fight, was one of many accolades that I had received personally from the soldiers on the ground that I supported. I had already accepted the responsibility of doing whatever it took to help out our guys on the ground. I would normally never hear the final outcome of any of the shootings that we were requested to do for the soldiers on the ground. Occasionally, like Staff Sgt. T., one of those soldiers would recognize our flight suits, and then see the telltale Coyote patch, that identified us as "one of those Apache guys". That private or Sergeant would make a deliberate effort to come and thank us personally for helping them out. There was no extra pay, no medals or anything tangible I could think of, that could match the feeling of being personally thanked by a soldier for saving them during a battle.

Worrying that the landing Chinooks would not brown out,
and collide, in the background.

91

Overview of landing zone and battle area of SOF team, Beast 54.
You can see the location of the Taliban machine gun nest
I destroyed with my 5 shot rocket attack.

Three uninjured detainees that were brought back to Bagram.
Steel beach is on the foreground.

Chapter 6

Go Guns

Lisa *I didn't dwell on the news. I received emails pretty regularly from him and he didn't leave anything out, which at times, I wished he would have. There were things that I didn't need to know and I never let the kids read everything. Most of the time I relayed information to them and would show them only previewed videos. His emails heightened my fear and I worried about things that I never would have thought of. There were things he should have told me after he was home safely, but he was Mr. Information with no filter from his brain to his mouth.*

Every morning brief we went too seemed to hold new surprises for us and this one was to be no different.

It was early in the morning and all the flight crews filed into the briefing room. As always, the briefing started with the weather then any special information or news that we needed to be aware of. Most of the news was about American soldiers killed by enemy gunfire or accidents. Then we were given the individual crew missions that were to be done that day. Basically, it was a lineup of who was flying what and where, then one of the Intel officers would give us the latest information on enemy activity in the locations we were flying to.

This day was rather odd because my mission was to escort 2 Chinook's to a place called the Ranch House, and the Chinook's were going to have a sling load. A sling load is cargo suspended by nylon rope below the aircraft, instead of inside it, because the load is too heavy, big or dangerous to be inside. Rarely did missions have sling loads, especially to the Ranch House.

Early in the first months of deployment the battalion commander for 10th Mountain had to jettison his sling load because it was swinging out of control. The load was a steel container that started spinning and swinging out of control underneath the Chinook. The Chinook crew tried several different maneuvers, while in route, to bring the sling load under control to no avail. They had to drop the load onto the desert floor below which caused the steel container to bust open and spread all sorts of military material on the ground. The two Chinooks landed and tried to salvage as much material as they could from the broken container. When they had cleaned up as much as they could, they called the Apache escorting them to fire high explosive and white phosphorous rockets to destroy as much of the remaining broken material as possible so the enemy could not use it.

The ranch house is, as the name implies, a ranch style house on the side of a mountain close to 11,000 feet above sea level. An interesting thing about the ranch house was there was no way to land safely on the actual house, nor was there any semblance of level ground anywhere near the house for any aircraft to attempt a landing. Every time a Blackhawk or a Chinook picked up or dropped off cargo and personnel, they would come to a hover over the flat roof of the house.

I, in the Apache helicopter, would circle overhead as they were doing their operations at the Ranch House. I was always amazed at how well the pilots kept their aircraft in a stable hover as people got off and on and transferred loads, especially when the winds were blowing across the mountains.

The Intel officer, in the morning briefing, told us that they had very credible information that there was an enemy heavy machine gun on our route that day. She told us that they had the actual grid coordinates and the altitude on the mountain where the gun was located. As she gave us the coordinates, I quickly copied them down on my knee board for the day's mission. She then continued to tell us that the Taliban had every intention of using that gun to shoot down one of our aircraft within the next 2 to 3 days.

This is the first time we'd ever gotten information like that, so obviously all the pilots and crew chiefs in the briefing room were talking amongst themselves. I was used to the Intel shop keeping information from us or not giving us any relevant information whatsoever, so I stood up to ask if they were going to either drop some bombs on that location or level that area with artillery.

She replied back, "No sir, we're going to wait and see what higher up wants to do".

I immediately replied back sarcastically, "Are they going to wait to prove the DSKH's (Soviet-made 14.5 mm antiaircraft machine gun) existence by the flaming Chinook at the bottom of the Valley?" Everybody in the room laughed except the Chinook pilots.

I immediately looked at the Chinook Pilot in Command (PIC) and told her it was nothing personal, she replied, "No problem". I looked back at the Intel officers and said, "In all seriousness, are you guys going to do anything about that DSKH?" I didn't mean to put her on the spot, but I was already fed up with the information we had been receiving and the lack of willpower higher-ups had to actually kill the enemy. After all, this was a war we were in, wasn't it?

I leaned over to Paul, my copilot for the day, and told him, "We'll do what needs to be done when we get in that area". I looked over to the two female Chinook pilots that were flying the mission and told them not to worry, "We'll do that Attack pilot thing". When the briefing was finished we all piled out of the room, mumbling under our breaths how headquarters was holding back on actually waging a war on the Taliban.

After preflighting the aircraft and lining up on the taxiway, I watched the Chinook hover over the position of the sling load they were going to take. It took a few minutes as the female flight crew of the Chinook precisely hovered over the cargo to let the ground personnel hook it up. Once that was accomplished, we got clearance from Bagram Tower and made our way eastbound.

When we departed Bagram, I realized the significance of this flight. The lead Chinook was being piloted by two female aviators. It never really dawned on me, here we were, going to a remote high mountain location, right past a known enemy threat, and two women were flying the lead Chinook with a sling load hanging underneath. I wasn't alarmed because I had already flown several missions with both of these women and to tell the truth, they were better than some of the gun pilots we had. I had no doubt in my mind as to the abilities and capabilities of these two female pilots, so I was not worried at all.

We made our way up the Konar river valley and as we approached Forward Operating Base (FOB) Asadabad, the lead Chinook called us on the radio to tell us they had a Combiner Transmission (C box) master warning light illuminate. Not knowing that much about Chinooks, I asked them if that was a bad thing. They replied that they were landing immediately at FOB Asadabad, as they were making an approach. They expertly set the sling load down then landed in front of it.

They were on the ground for a few seconds when they called back and said the light had gone out. Their crew chief thought it was just merely a short in one of the wires, or an anomaly, so the Chinook immediately lifted off with the sling load following them into the air. We flew north over the town of Asadabad then made the left turn westbound along the Pech river valley.

A few miles further, I called up to the lead Chinook and told them that we were approaching the suspected DSKH site. I would fly ahead of the 2 Chinooks and shoot several rockets and fire the gun at the known location, just to make sure nobody would surprise us. The two Chinooks replied back that it sounded like a great idea and they would both stay to the north side of the valley while I did my Apache thing on the south side.

With the impromptu plan briefed to all involved we inputted the coordinates of the known DSKH site. Paul "slaved" the targeting sight system to the coordinates and looked around for the machine gun itself. I lined up my rocket attack symbology and then actioned up my rockets. Paul actioned his rockets and I confirmed that all the proper attack symbology was displayed.

I maneuvered the aircraft to line up the shot as Paul looked through the magnified targeting system to make sure there were no innocent sheep herders or livestock in the area and also try to locate the actual gun itself, if it really was there. I reconfirmed all the switches were correct and squeezed the trigger. The electric squibs fired on the rocket and it came to life. It made a loud swoosh as it soared straight ahead of us towards the ridgeline as I followed the smoke trail. At first, I thought the rocket was going to fly over the intended location, and then noticed what appeared to be a house on the far side of the ridgeline. I thought the rocket went too far and hoped it wasn't going to hit the house. The rocket looked like it was flying right over the spot I intended, then as if by magic, I saw an explosion right where I planned. Paul started shooting the area with the gun as I made a right turn. We flew within 500 meters of the spot and both Paul and I looked out the left window to see if there was anything we might have destroyed. All I could make out were rocks and a few small trees. I started setting up for another attack run when the Chinooks called and said they were continuing westbound. One attack run was all we got.

I pulled in max power to catch up to the two Chinooks. Several miles westbound, in the Pech River Valley, is Camp Blessing located at a "Y" where the Pech River Valley veers off to the southwest and the Waygal

Valley splits off to the north. The Waygal Valley leads north deeper into the Hindu Kush. As we made our way past Camp Blessing, the mountains really began to rise dramatically on both sides of the Valley. We headed north for about 15 miles before making a right turn to the east, entering the valley that the Ranch House overlooked. The mountains here reminded me of Yosemite national Park, only these mountains were scraping the sky at close to 16,000 feet, with snow still lingering all year long. Looking out all around us, there was no way of making a successful emergency landing anywhere. There wasn't a flat piece of earth anywhere to be found.

A few storm clouds had started building around the mountains and I got a little worried that we may be cut off from the valley when we returned this way.

We turned into the valley where the Ranch House was and all three aircraft started climbing. Even as high as we were, the Ranch House was even higher still. The first Chinook lined up their approach and expertly delivered the sling load to the flat roof top of the Ranch House. Once the sling load was gently placed on the roof, so as not to collapse it, the two female pilots maneuvered the Chinook around to place only the rear wheels on top of the house, which is called a tailgate landing. The crew chief lowered the ramp and a bunch of soldiers lined up to offload the rest of the equipment that was inside the Chinook. As I was circling overhead, I couldn't help but think how brave and skilled the two female Chinook pilots were. I was also amazed at how much power those Chinook's had.

My Apache, which only had two pilots and two engines, was not capable of coming to a hover at these altitudes much less carry a sling load.

The second Chinook lined up on the Ranch House and did the same thing as the first one. The sling load mission was going along smoothly, almost too smoothly. Once both Chinook's had finished their offloading of equipment, we made our way south toward Camp Blessing and the Pech River Valley.

Passing by Camp Blessing, as we entered the Pech River Valley heading eastbound, the radios came alive with a call from a vehicle patrol base near where we had fired our rockets and gun at the possible DSKH sight earlier. The vehicle patrol base asked us if I was the Apache that shot at the top of the valley about an hour prior. I told him, "Yes that was me who did the shooting earlier, why?"

He said that as soon as I had fired on that area they intercepted radio calls between the Taliban asking if the gun had been damaged. I told him that we had coordinates of a possible DSKH heavy machine gun in that area. He said that whatever it was we shot at brought about a lot of commotion and radio chatter throughout the entire valley. As we flew by the base, I told him the commotion was probably a good indicator that there really was a DSKH in the area. I gave him the coordinates, and made a hint that they should call in an artillery strike to that location. I wished him good luck, as we continued eastbound out of radio range with him.

A few miles later we were over the city of Asadabad. We made a right turn along the Konar River and flew past FOB Asadabad. As we continued south, I was thinking it was going to be a short day. No sooner had I thought that, the lead Chinook called out on the radio that they had another "C" box warning light illumination. She said they were making an immediate landing directly in front of them which was on the bank of the Konar river. I watched as she made an approach to a small field just south of a group of homes. Chinook number two followed them down to a safe landing; so much for a short and easy day.

I circled overhead at 200 feet and watched them shut down both aircraft. The field they landed in was about 500 meters south of the group of homes and about 300meters to the west of the main road. We were only 15 miles north of Jalalabad.

With both aircraft safely on the ground, it was time to come up with options. Hopefully, the warning light was just a short circuit in the wiring, as before. I called to the Chinooks and asked if they knew what the problem was. They called back saying the light was real.

As I circled overhead, out of the corner of my eye I saw movement near the homes. I squinted, trying to focus at what the movement was and then my heart skipped a beat.

Several hundred local Afghan villagers were running toward the aircraft and there was no telling what was going through their minds. I assumed they thought the Chinooks were there to give away goods to them. Since there were only the two female pilots with the two crew chiefs managing the guns, I couldn't open fire but I also knew that I couldn't let the villagers get close to them because Taliban soldiers could be hiding within the group, seizing the opportunity to take female American prisoners. I started thinking of what my options were to stop the mob before they reached the 2 aircraft. I also knew I wasn't justified in using any weapons on innocent civilians because that would make great propaganda for the Taliban.

I circled around and commenced a dive to less than 20ft above the ground, flying at 120 knots. I lined up my flight path directly in front of the approaching crowd and I placed my thumb on the red button on top of my cyclic and pushed down several times letting out a string of flares in hopes of getting the villagers' attention and stop them from advancing any further. The flares bounced off the ground and arched upwards toward the mob. I pulled out of the low level run, circled around, and let out more flares. The villagers got the message and stopped less than 200 meters away from the Chinooks.

I radioed to the Chinooks about the mob stopping then relayed to Jalalabad, which was not more than a few miles to the south over a ridgeline, and told them the Chinooks were on the ground due to a maintenance problem.

The controller at Jalalabad airfield told us to keep circling and provide cover until a maintenance rescue team could be assembled and deployed.

We circled over the stricken aircraft for an hour and a half and finally, after not hearing any news from Jalalabad, called back to let them know we had less than 15 minutes of gas left. The crew chiefs and the pilots of both Chinooks had established a secure perimeter around the aircraft, but there were only eight of them on the ground with hundreds of villagers still watching from a distance. Jalalabad radioed back they still didn't have the maintenance team ready. I told them they needed to get someone overhead to relieve us soon, as we were running low on fuel.

As always, the relief Apache showed up just in time for us to use the last of our fuel to get back to Jalalabad.

On the ground, the pilots and crew chiefs were preparing to spend the night in the aircraft. It was several hours later when the maintenance rescue team arrived. The Chinook that arrived carried a maintenance crew, along with a security team of infantry soldiers to protect all the mechanics and aircraft for the overnight stay.

Overhead, a flight of A-10 Warthogs would maintain a vigil throughout the night.

When we arrived in Afghanistan, all of us were issued a bottle of anti-malaria pills. We were told to take one pill every day until the bottle was empty and then we would be issued another bottle of pills. We were to take the pills the entire year we were in country. I knew I didn't want to get malaria, so I diligently started taking my pills every day. At first, my stomach started feeling really bad but I figured I would get used to the pills after a week or so. Then I started to have some really weird and unsettling dreams which I attributed to being away from my family and in a war zone. After two weeks of stomach aches and waking up in the middle of night, I decided I would only take the pills whenever I went to Jalalabad. I talked to several of the other pilots and found out I was not the only one that was having a problem with the anti-malaria pills.

I had completely forgotten about taking the pills when I was sent to Jalalabad.

A few weeks after this event, I found out that one of the crew chiefs, that had stayed overnight working on the Chinooks, had come down with malaria.

I started to rethink my idea of not taking the pills and the possible consequences of doing that. It's interesting to think that back in the United States nobody really takes a second thought about getting malaria. I knew I only had a few months left in the country, and I certainly didn't want to go home with a possible life-threatening disease, so I started to take the pills again, and the upset stomach, and the weird dreams came right back, as if on cue. It was also at this time that the Sergeant Major with the 10th Mountain division realized that more than half of his troops were not taking the anti-malaria pills. So the Army did what the Army does best and they *ordered* everyone to start taking their pills. Whether the pills were being consumed by the soldiers or not was irrelevant because the bottles were being ordered and the empty bottles were being exchanged for full ones.

Later that night, the Quick Reactionary Force (QRF) Apaches, out of Jalalabad, flew back to the suspected DSHK gun site. They ended up finding the gun, right where I had shot earlier, and killed close to 20 Taliban fighters that were hiding in caves around the gun site.

Chinook with C-box problem that landed next to the Konar river.
The local villagers came from the area at the top of the picture.

Flare launch over the Konar river valley. Used to keep the locals
away from downed chinook, without firing a live round.

Chapter 7

Apache Rescue

Lisa   *While he was gone an opportunity to work part time at our church came up and I jumped on it. I had been out of the working world for a long time, but with his cut in pay due to leaving, his civilian job, it was better to be safe than sorry. The cut in pay wasn't too bad though since we were supporting one less person, but it was still stressful all the same. The most stressful thing though was the daily task of doing everything and taking the kids everywhere. I instantly became a single mom. It was frustrating when the kids had to be at two different places at the same time. Many people offered their help and support but I didn't like to ask for anything. I felt like I would be a pest if I asked anyone for anything, so it all fell on me.*

When I found out that I was being deployed to Afghanistan, I did everything I could to make sure I would be able to take as many pictures and video of the tour as possible. I wanted to document it for my children and future generations to see what their "dad" did during the great war on terror.

I had learned years earlier from my time on active duty to take pictures of everyone and everything. I would look back at some of those old pictures and reminisce about the "good 'ole days". I would then wish that I had taken even more pictures of my friends and things we did back then.

I had a standard digital camera and an 8mm digital camcorder. So far through the tour I had taken videos from out the window as I flew along.

The Apache has its own video recorder built into the sighting systems but the "hard drive" system that was installed had lots of problems. More times than not, it would not work. It was particularly frustrating because we wouldn't have any indication that it wasn't recording until after we landed and by then it was too late. I had gotten accustomed to just setting up my camera on the dash and relying on that video.

It was sad that a privately purchased, off the shelf, camcorder was more reliable than a several thousand dollar system the government purchased to install in a multi-million dollar aircraft.

A pilot from Idaho, who was attached to us, had shown me some video he had taken while riding his motorcycle back home. It was taken by a camera attached to his helmet and you could see the perspective of him riding in the mountains. I thought that was pretty cool. He had mentioned that he was going to order one of those "lipstick" cameras and try to mount it outside the aircraft and get a different view, so I told him to order me one also.

Several weeks had gone by before we received the cameras. That pilot had gone on his leave so I was stuck with trying to figure out how to mount the camera, and how to hook it up to the aircraft's audio and my own camcorder inside the cockpit. The whole new setup sat in my room for a few weeks. I tried several times to figure out the myriad of wires that needed to be connected to make this camera system work, but failed to either get a picture or audio or both. Finally one of the other pilots helped me out and I was really happy that we got the setup to record audio and video. The next order of business was to find a place to mount the camera on the Apache and make sure it got a good view that didn't compromise the safety of the aircraft in anyway.

Finally, on October 4th 2006 I was on quick reactionary force (QRF) again. I had decided that I would quit procrastinating and mount the camera somehow. After my preflight I put all my flight gear on the wing for quick access should I be called to launch. I found a spot on the left side main landing gear step where I could run the camera wires inside the fairing and into the vent which was also on that side and then hook it straight to my camcorder in the cockpit.

We were more than halfway through our tour and people started to get complacent around Bagram. One thing about the military, if you don't keep people busy then mischief is sure to follow. We were in a combat zone and yet the powers that be felt obligated to keep everyone safe, whether they were outside "the wire" (fence) or inside "the wire". It was a noble cause, but sometimes things were better left alone. Over the previous few days the Military Police (MP's) were ordered to give out "citations" to any individual that was caught walking around the base without an official Army issued neon green or red reflective belt.

In the mind of someone who never left the confines and safety of the base, the most dangerous thing that could happen was the chance of getting hit by a vehicle while crossing the one main street on the base. Therefore if everyone was ordered to wear a highly reflective safety belt then no one would get injured while in the combat zone.

The sergeant major had seen fit that if you were caught without one of these highly visible neon green reflective belts on your person, then you were deemed unsafe, and must therefore be punished. So he had the base police on high alert to stop and issue a citation, on the spot, to anyone caught walking around the base (in a combat zone) without a wearing a reflective belt.

Obviously, those of us who regularly left the confines of the base to fight the good fight were pretty upset at this new law. There really wasn't anything that we could do to not wear the reflective belt, and not get a citation. So we did what most everyone else did, we complained every chance we could to whoever agreed with us, and drove on.

On this day though, after finally installing my new "bullet cam", as my lipstick camera would later be named, we decided to strap a reflective belt to the tail boom of our alert aircraft and take pictures of it. We had planned on making copies of it and then post them around the base as a display of our rebellion to this ludicrous Law.

After we took a few pictures and laughed at our mini rebellion, we left the reflective belt on the tailboom, and departed to the chow hall to get something to eat.

While eating lunch, our ICOM radios came alive with an "immediate Launch" order for the Alert QRF Apaches, ME!

This was very unusual because we had not been called out like this before. I started a quick run to our Command Post (CP) to get the real story on this "launch" order. When I rounded the last corner facing our command post, I was met by one of our crew chiefs whom had my M4 in his hands and said he would follow me to the aircraft. He said that a convoy was ambushed and we were ordered to launch immediately.

We both ran across "Steel Beach". Steel Beach was the area known to twist ankles and tweak knees. It was the part of the ramp area that had stamped corrugated steel, instead of concrete, that was left by the Soviets when they occupied the airfield. The corrugation had a perfect 3 inch wide flat spot followed by a 3 inch wide groove that ran the length of about 200 feet. If you were good, you could walk on the high ridge, one foot in front of the other (like a balance beam) and not get your foot caught in the groove and possibly twist an ankle. Steel beach had claimed its fair share of injuries so far.

I came up to steel beach and knew things were serious when I saw one of our crew chiefs in the pilot's seat (mine), and already had the auxiliary power unit (APU) and most of the systems up and running. I also saw that the other QRF Apache was already at 100% rpm's. One of the crew chiefs said that the pilot of the other Apache had gotten the information and would brief me as soon as I was up and ready to takeoff.

I looked over to one of the other crew chiefs, and saw him give me a puzzled look, as he held the "Safety Reflective Belt" in his hands, that he had taken off of my aircraft. He looked at me and shrugged his shoulders. I just gave him a thumbs up and a quick smile, and then put on my body armor and survival vest as I hopped into my aircraft.

As soon as I got on the radio, Doc called me and said we were cleared to depart from our present position, as opposed to taxiing out like a conventional airplane as we normally did. That got me spooled up even more. We had never received a clearance to depart directly from our parking position before. Bagram airfield was a very busy, major airport for the entire northern sector of Afghanistan. It had arrival and departing aircraft 24 hours a day which ranged from civilian contract DC-9's to F-15 fighter jets to Apache attack helicopters. The Air Force controllers were always busy trying to de-conflict the variety of aircraft, and work with the different speeds that they all used. It also included working with most of the night time traffic having no lights turned on whatsoever, due to tactical reasons.

We both departed straight east out of Bagram then Doc told me that a convoy had been ambushed in the Tagab Valley and the last word was there were in excess of 200 Taliban surrounding them. We plugged in the coordinates and saw that the location was only 15 miles to our front, or the northern end of the Tagab Valley.

We made sure our weapons were turned on but couldn't do a test fire since we were headed straight to the fight without flying by the normal test fire area.

We discussed the shooting priorities, and made up some semblance of a plan before arriving at the coordinates given. A few minutes passed as we flew over the coordinates and sure enough, nothing.

We flew over a vacant portion of desert and no one was in sight. So the copilot for the other Apache, started calling on the radio to try and find anyone out there that was in need of rescuing.

We both reconfirmed the coordinates that were given to us and after several attempts of calling in the blind we finally got a very faint response. We couldn't make out what was said, so we kept on calling and then listening but it was still too faint to make out. This went on for a good 5 minutes, which seemed like an eternity. I finally saw a lone Humvee in the field we originally flew over, but I couldn't tell if he was the one calling us on the radio. I flew over him several times to see if he was the one in need of rescuing, but I could tell there was definitely no one shooting at him. In fact there was no one within a good mile of him. He was just sitting out in the middle the desert, watching us as we flew by.

I heard Leo calling on the other radios in attempt to get a hold of anyone to respond. I finally had enough of flying around and decided I was going to land in front of the Humvee to get a face to face talk to find out who needed help and where they were located.

I asked Paul to read out the before landing checklist as I started my turn on final approach to a spot about 50 meters in front of the lone Humvee.

As I made my final approach to land in the field in front of the Humvee, Doc called me on the radio to tell me that they had made contact with the ground element and had them in sight. I waved off my approach, and added power. I then saw that Doc's Apache was just south of my position by about 2 miles. He was circling a compound and there were several Toyota HiLux and Ford Ranger pickups on the road under him.

Doc said that there were Afghan National Army (ANA) soldiers on the ground pointing and shooting at an Orchard just east of their position across a small canyon. The person on the other end of the radio could be heard faintly telling us about an Orchard to their east that they were receiving fire from.

I looked over to where Doc was flying and sure enough there was an Orchard across a small canyon and it just happened to be to the east of the soldiers on the ground shooting in that direction. Doc and I made a quick plan for him to fly over the orchard and see if he could spot any Taliban. I fell in trail behind him and discussed with my copilot, to keep an eye on them, and if they took fire, we would immediately open fire and cover them as they flew by.

Doc lined up and sure enough as he flew over the orchard, the ground below him erupted in smoke and dust. Several Taliban opened fire on him. I was already lined up, and lit off a White Phosphorous rocket in the area below Doc's Apache, to suppress the gunfire. That white phosphorous rocket impacted the road short of where I wanted it to hit. I mumbled "Shit" under my breath because I didn't take my time and line up the shot properly. I turned left slightly to avoid overflying the orchard. My copilot called out for me to bank right so he could start shooting the 30 mm gun into the orchard. He fired off 2, 10 round bursts, each one shook the aircraft. He was shooting directly to the right from the direction we were flying.

Finally, we had the enemy in sight, with the "good guys" covered, and started the business of pummeling the Taliban.

We circled around and this time, made a deliberate attack run on the known location of the Taliban in the orchard. Doc would make a run in and light the orchard up with high explosive (HE) rockets and I would follow up with the same pounding, in just a slightly different location of the orchard. After my second attack run, as I flew past the orchard and a house that was located on the north end of the orchard, I looked down to see a person squatting down by the door. We flew by so fast that I really couldn't tell if he had a gun in his hands or not. As I was watching Doc in the other Apache shooting up the orchard, I started thinking that this was just too easy.

Then as if on cue, I heard a transmission over the radio that sent chills up my spine. Vandal 1-6, the convoy commander that had called us in, asked if we were in sight of him, and if we could provide attack support to him.

"OH SHIT", I thought. What the hell is going on here? Who had we just fired up, and where was Vandal 1-6? If that wasn't "him" below us, watching us fire up the orchard, then who were we providing cover for below?

Vandal 1-6 called again, stating that he couldn't see us shooting at the enemy to their front. He was as perplexed, as I was, as to what was happening, or in his case, not happening.

Leo called him back and requested a situation report again. Mainly he and I wanted a positive location as to Vandal's whereabouts in this long valley. Now that we had good communications with each other, we had to positively identify who was who, and where everyone was.

Vandal stated that he was at the southern end of the valley, or about 5 miles southeast of our present position. Vandal reiterated his situation. He was a ground convoy commander with Humvee's that had been ambushed, and needed to evacuate to the north on the main road of the valley.

Both Doc and I made a turn to the southeast and started flying in that direction. Doc took the middle of the valley and headed southeast as fast as he could. I took-up a wingman position to his right, along the southern wall of the Tagab valley. We followed the road heading southeast, low level and with full military power to get to the new location as fast as possible.

Along the way, I discussed with my copilot who was it that we had just "lit up", and secretly hoped no friendlies were hurt at the site. As I watched Doc's Apache fly over some orchards just east of the main road, the whole world lit up underneath him. I saw RPG's fly up behind Doc's Apache, and then explode in the air slightly above his altitude. I saw muzzle flashes and dust being kicked up by all the gunfire directed at him. I called out, "I got them in sight", and yanked hard left on the cyclic. I lined up my attack symbology on the orchard where the gunfire had just come from. I lit off 3 high explosive rockets in quick succession, into the orchard, and my copilot started firing away with the 30 mm chain gun, as we flew over at 200 feet and close to 200 mph. Right then, Vandal called out on the radio that it was a good shot. Doc made a hard right turn to make another run at the orchard from a different direction. I saw him fire off a salvo of rockets and bullets as I pulled up hard into a climbing right turn. I traded off my speed for altitude, as I lined up on the orchard with the sun behind me. I fired off another salvo of rockets and bullets at the tree line around the orchard, and at footpaths that lined the area.

On the ground Vandal 1-6 and his convoy were cheering and hollering at their "big brothers" coming in to save the day.

Doc and I traded attack runs from all different directions. First at the orchard, and then all the footpath's around the location where Taliban soldiers were shooting from. On several run-ins, I looked out my side window and saw some of the Taliban shooting at us with AK-47s.

It was interesting to see the muzzle flashes directed straight at me as we flew by. It was surreal to think that there were a lot of people down there that wanted to kill me.

On the ground, Vandal started loading up the Afghan Army and his own soldiers. He headed northwest up the main highway as fast as they could get those Humvee's to go. Doc and I had made several runs at the orchard, when I noticed that the convoy was about a mile up the road, driving like they were possessed. I called to Doc and asked if we should stay with the convoy or continue our attack in the area. Doc called back and said we were staying with the convoy. That was all I needed to hear. I made a turn to start up the highway behind the convoy. I dropped down to about 50 feet, adding maximum power and flew over their heads as low as was safe to show them that we were still with them.

A few miles up the road was another small village that was very near to the first location we were shooting at earlier. Since the road in front of the convoy was clear, Doc and I circled the small cluster of homes looking for any signs of the Taliban trying to set up an ambush.

On the north side of the cluster of homes was the original, small convoy of Toyota and Ford pickups that had separated from Vandal 1-6 during the first ambush. We contacted the incoming convoy and alerted them to their separated vehicles. They were parked on the other side of the village of homes they were approaching. I guess Vandal and the convoy were moving so fast, and the Humvee's were making so much noise that nobody in the Humvee's could hear us, because we got no response.

I found out later that they were all hanging on to whatever they could, because the roads were so rough. They did not want to get hurt inside their own vehicles, nor lose control at the speeds they were driving, on the poor excuse for roads they were on.

When the convoy approached the village, they had to slow down considerably to negotiate their vehicles in between the tall buildings. Doc and his Apache took up a low orbit over the neighborhood while I gained altitude and covered him from a few hundred feet above. As the convoy made its way through the homes we periodically lost sight of some of the individual vehicles due to the narrowness of the road.

Doc circled to the northeast of the neighborhood, over the orchard we had shot up previously. As Vandal 1-6, and his convoy, made their way through the neighborhood, the radios erupted again with him calling out, "They are shooting from the rooftops!"

I happened to be in a perfect position to roll in on the homes at the north end of the cluster as the last vehicle from the convoy was leaving. I lined up on one of the homes, and was about to squeeze off a high explosive rocket when I started thinking, "I don't see anybody outright shooting at them from any of those rooftops" The last vehicle was definitely clear of where I was about to shoot, so I could've made a righteous shot without fear of hitting one of our own vehicles. I decided at the last second not to shoot.

Even though we were in the middle of a fight, I still had to make good, sound decisions as to when, or when not to shoot. When all was said and done, there were still human beings down there that wanted no part of this war. We are Americans, and we know better than to go shooting and killing just because we can. I had my own children at home to think about, and I thanked God every day that we lived in America, and didn't have to deal with an all out war in our own backyard.

The main convoy, with Vandal 1-6, linked up again with their original vehicles all stopped to make sure everybody was accounted for before they moved on.

Doc called me on the radio and told me about the next village the convoy was about to drive through. Apparently there were numerous individuals with AK-47s lined up on both sides of the street. Doc said that it looked to him like everybody was up to no good. I looked over at him about a mile north of where I was. He was making a low pass and dropping flares over the village he was talking about. My copilot and I agreed that we would make several passes as fast and low as we dared, as a show of force before the ground convoy made its way through.

I lined up my run and saw several individuals start to make their way underneath the awnings that bordered the street. This village had small buildings on both sides lining the street which was a very wide dirt road leading from one end of the town to the other. It made me think of what a town in the old West would've looked like from the air. The so-called street running through the town was about 100 feet wide, as opposed to the rest of the dirt highway before and after this village. There were shops instead of homes lining both sides.

As I was lining up to make the run in from one end of town to the other, one of the individuals underneath the entrance to a building, pulled something out from underneath his man dress. I started my attack run and was thinking, "Great. This guy is going to pull something out. That will justify me putting a rocket right where he's standing." As I lined up my attack symbology for a rocket run, I saw a bright flash of light from where the individual was standing.

I slowly started squeezing the trigger while reconfirming my attack symbology was all lined up on the individual I was about to kill. Just before I made that last millimeter movement on the trigger I noticed all the guy was doing was holding up a mirror and reflecting the sun back at me. I went ahead and continued my run in, but instead of killing him and his cohorts with a rocket, I reached down with my thumb, on the cyclic, and fired off a salvo of flares.

It was pretty funny to see those guy's eyes open wide and then run inside the building, thinking I was shooting at them.

We both made several runs over the village shooting off flares, as a show of force, to let them all know not to mess with our convoy.

We called Vandal 1-6 and made sure they knew about the town they were going to roll through, and all the suspect individuals that were no longer lining the streets, thanks to our flybys, and flare drops. Vandal called back saying they knew about the village and that nobody there was up to any good. This small village was no more than about 200 yards long and at the north end was the final goal. The FOB was within a 1 mile reach.

The convoy made it through the village without any incident. I was thankful those individuals decided not to attack the convoy. Doc and I were lined up, ready to destroy the entire village should anyone have started shooting at the convoy. He was lined up to attack the west side of the road, and I was lined up to attack the east side. It would've been a big mess, but we would have done whatever it took to protect Vandal and his men.

Firing up an entire village was not something we would have looked forward to doing. The guys in the village may have been bad, but it would not have made good news if we had to level an entire village.

The convoy continued about another quarter mile past the village as they passed a motorcycle that was parked on the side of the road. It looked like an old 1969 model Honda CB 100. It had the old chrome fenders and pseudo-chrome gas tank. We had seen these motorcycles all over the country. It's like the Taliban issued everyone this exact same motorcycle.

Right then the radio screamed to life with Vandal 1-6 yelling out, "In the fields! In the fields"! The owner of the motorcycle was one of the people from the village and had decided to start his own war in the field next to the road, and the convoy. The convoy fired off some shots as I rolled in and asked my copilot if he could see the shooter. My copilot said that he had him in his sights and was going to shoot him with the 30 mm gun. He started shooting away as I was straining to see where he was shooting at. He called out that he got him, and was looking for anybody else in the field.

As the convoy crossed a dry creek, on one of the very few intact bridges in the country, my copilot called out to me saying that he thought he saw someone underneath the bridge. I circled around and lined up again in preparation to shoot whoever was underneath that bridge, if they were up to no good. As we got closer, my copilot started laughing and told me to never mind, it was just a horse.

I thought for a second, poor horse. He probably heard the shooting down the valley slowly getting louder as we came closer, and then two helicopters circled overhead while about 15 vehicles came across the bridge making a bunch of noise that he probably wasn't used to.

A quarter of a mile past the bridge, the convoy reached the top of the hill and arrived at their destination. It was an Afghan National Police checkpoint at the north end of the Tagab Valley.

Vandal 1-6 made his last transmission on the radio to say that they were all safe at the FOB (Forward Operating Base). He also told us that they would go back and pick up the RANGER, whenever they got the chance. My copilot immediately said on the intercom, "The Ranger? What Ranger is he talking about?" I told him about a Ford Ranger pickup truck that did not make it up the last hill before the engine quit. All its oil spilled on the road from a bullet that had ruptured its oil tank. The Ford Ranger pickup truck was sitting just below the crest of the hill with a large black spot growing out from underneath it.

For a second he thought that the convoy had left a soldier, or more specifically, a U.S. Army Ranger behind.

With the convoy safely at the checkpoint we continued circling the area looking for something else to shoot. That's when we noticed, the motorcycle of the last insurgent we killed, was left on the road. Since the owner of that motorcycle no longer needed it we decided to do some target practice. We made several gun runs on the motorcycle taking turns shooting it. After several attempts the last burst we fired hit the motorcycle. Apparently we hit the gas tank as the motorcycle exploded in a huge ball of fire and smoke. It was one of those Hollywood explosions that had a small mushroom cloud rising over the now destroyed motorcycle. And as luck would have it the tape on my camcorder had finished a few seconds before the explosion.

A little over an hour after we launched from Bagram, Doc and his Apache led us both back home. We still had about an hour's worth of fuel left in our aircraft. I was completely out of rockets, and was very low on 30 mm. Doc and his Apache were about the same. We both discussed how close we had come to almost running out of ammunition in this one-hour fight. We were both very happy that the convoy had made it safely to its destination, before we ran out of ammunition.

The flight back to Bagram was not even 15 minutes long. That's how close the valley was to Bagram. We did our normal landing back at Bagram, and taxied into our parking spots that we had left earlier. I was guided into my parking spot by my crew chief, who crossed his arms, indicating to set my brakes, and start my shutdown. With the fight being so close to home, the crew chiefs monitored our radio traffic, and the fighting, as it happened. It was no surprise that all of them had come out to greet us as we landed.

I finished my shutdown and hopped out of the aircraft, handing my crew chief my M4, and my knee board. Paul had already gotten out and made his way to the other Apache, which had parked next to us. Apparently, since they shut down about a minute before me, several of the crew chiefs and civilian mechanics immediately spotted several bullet holes in Doc's aircraft.

I quickly walked around my aircraft looking for any obvious signs of bullet holes, but saw none. I grabbed my camera and ran over to where Doc, Paul and Leo were standing, looking at all the bullet holes in Doc's aircraft.

All four of us and the other soldiers standing around were happy and proud of the fight, the convoy, and the bullet holes.

I guess to the average person, getting shot at by so many people with so many different types of weapons would probably be a little unnerving. But to us gun pilots, the satisfaction of saving a convoy, and having an hour's worth of shooting, and killing the enemy was a dream come true.

Having bullet holes in our aircraft was more a badge of honor than anything else. We took several pictures of Doc's aircraft with all of us standing and pointing at the bullet holes. I was actually kind of proud that my aircraft did not have any bullet holes in it, or so I thought. All four of us were happy as could be at the bullet holes in Doc's aircraft and the outcome of the mission!

I walked back to our command post and started filling out the information on the aircraft computer, so that the crew chiefs could get the aircraft ready for the next flight.

Just as I had started filling out the paperwork one of the crew chiefs came in and told me that my aircraft had been hit also. I looked up at him and said, "Real funny, you're just messing with me aren't you?"

He said, "No, go out there and look for yourself, they're changing the blade right now" I got up from my seat and headed out the door to see for myself. The crew chief walked all the way out there with me and said that I had taken a bullet hole in the one of the Main rotor blades.

Sure enough, as I walked to my aircraft, the mechanics had one of the cranes hooked up to my rotor blade. I couldn't believe it, I asked them to wait a second while I grabbed my camera and then asked the crew chief where the bullet hole was. He pointed to a small, about a quarter inch, white spot on the bottom of the blade. I had to strain my eyes to see it, that's how small it was. I climbed onto the back of the aircraft so I could look at the top of the blade. As soon as I could see the top of the blade, there it was. The fiberglass was already peeling back from the top of the composite blade where the bullet had exited. We both started looking a lot closer over every square inch of that aircraft but we found no other bullet holes.

After we finished up the paperwork for our flights, we all headed back to our B hut to see the video from my camera that I had hooked up. In the middle of our B hut we had set up a makeshift movie theater. Up until then, we either watched movies or played Xbox with a projector and surround sound system, on an 8 foot high by 10 foot wide space on the wall that we had painted white. We hooked up my camera to play the videotape of the mission we had just completed. As we started the tape, a few other pilots and crew chiefs had gathered in our makeshift theater to watch.

The video started and there was no sound at first. Then someone reached over to turn the volume up. We heard Paul and me talking over the intercom, and the radio transmissions between Doc's Apache and mine, as we flew out to the ambush location. As it is with a bunch of pilots, critiques were more than abundant. For about the first 10 minutes we were just flying around and trying to make contact with Vandal 1-6. Everybody got quiet as we got to the point where Doc was about to make his attack on the first orchard. You could have heard a pin drop, as I started rolling in and lining up to shoot the first rocket. The gun was clearly visible on the right side of the screen, as it was moving with Paul's head, as it was supposed to. The rest of the screen was filled with the landscape that we were flying over.

The sound of the first rocket firing was pretty cool, nothing Hollywood about it. Just the standard swoosh that we were all used to as the rocket was fired. What happened next almost brought tears to everybody's eyes. Paul called for me to roll back right so he could shoot the gun. As we were all mesmerized to the screen . . . the gun fired off, in full 5.1 surround sound with a powered subwoofer. The sound of the gun was incredible! Everybody stood up and cheered every time we fired the gun, the sound was that good!

For the enlisted soldiers, they were all excited just to see what a real fight was like in the country side. They did not usually have an opportunity to see this, due to their jobs on the base fixing the aircraft that we pilots continually broke for them. Everybody sat still for close to an hour and watched the entire length of the flight tape. There was only one other type of movie that could command that much attention from a bunch of Army soldiers so far away from home.

After watching the video, everyone told me they wanted their own copy. As for me, I now had the job of transferring the videotape to DVDs.

Making the video had another purpose for me. I was making an edited copy for Vandal 1-6 so hopefully he could show it to all of his soldiers. Plus, I was hoping he would show the other soldiers in the area of operations (AO). This would allow them to see what the Apache guys see and hear whenever we show up to support them on the ground.

I hoped to use the DVD as a training tool for the ground soldiers (since I was still an instructor pilot). For others to see and hear what they sounded like when they were talking to us overhead, supporting them.

As an added bonus at the end of the video, I added several pictures of all four of us pilots that were on the mission, and still pictures of the Valley, along with the soundtrack "Everybody was Kung Fu fighting!"

A few days later, while I was out on a mission, Vandal 1-6 stopped by our command post on Bagram airfield. He wanted to stop by and thank the 4 pilots that had come to his rescue in the Tagab Valley. One of the other pilots, that was not on that mission, told him our names and let him know that we had a DVD of that day's events. He started showing Vandal 1-6 the video on our TV in the command post. He said that Vandal was in awe as to the clarity of the video, and the sound and the events that played out that day. He said that Vandal was asking, "How we knew exactly where to shoot" since you could not see that detail on the TV. But overall, every time he saw shooting in the video, he confirmed that was exactly where the enemy shooting was coming from.

Vandal 1-6 was extremely thankful that we showed up and did what we did for him and all the other soldiers that were in his convoy.

About a week later, I was in the Jalalabad chow hall one evening. The good thing about our flight suits as Army aviators is that the enlisted and all the other soldiers know who we are and how few we are. As I sat at a table a Major stopped by and asked if he could sit and eat with us. Obviously, wanting to be friendly, we all said yes. The Major and I started talking about the Tagab Valley ambush, and all the events that happened that day. Major Bumm was the commander for Vandal 1-6, and all of the other soldiers that were in country to train the Afghan National Army. As soon as he told me that, I remembered that I had a copy of the DVD, from the ambush, that I wanted to give to Vandal 1-6. I told Maj. Bumm about this, and he said that he would be happy to take that DVD to him, so he could show it to the other soldiers as a training tool. Major Bumm then made a comment, off the cuff, that he would like to make a copy of the DVD and send it to his dad. I told him sure; I figured his dad was a normal American, who supported his son over here, and all the other troops fighting in this war. We all swapped stories for a while longer then said our goodbyes.

A week later, I was back at Bagram airbase in the 10th Mountain command post. I was telling one of the Intelligence Captain's about meeting some Major from the ground training forces over at Jalalabad. The Captain asked me to repeat that major's name for him one more time to clarify it in his mind. I told him yeah some Major . . . I think his name was Major Bumm or something like that. That Captain cracked a big smile and asked me, "Do you know who that Majors dad is?" With a blank look on my face, I told the Captain "I don't know?"

He told me that Maj. Bumm's dad was the senior general for the United States Army National Guard. I then cracked a smile saying, "Well I guess Maj. Bumm's dad was not just some normal American dad, supporting his son over here". He then told me, "Maj. Bumm works in the Pentagon this very day!" Paul immediately blurted out, "Oh great, the Pentagon is watching our video and listening to "everybody was kung fu fighting!"

We all busted out laughing, envisioning in our minds, what that must look like, a bunch of senior military generals, possibly briefing President George Bush, in a dark, super secure bunker deep beneath the bowels of the Pentagon watching a combat video, which I had sent. All the while tapping their feet to the music of "everybody was kung fu fighting!"

It took about another month before I finally met Vandal 1-6 in person. We both talked for what seemed like hours about everything that was going on, but mainly about that day, October 4th, when our two lives crossed. Vandal kept reiterating how brave all us Apache guys were. He said that every time we flew over some location where there was a lot of Taliban shooting, there would be an eruption of RPG's fired at us as we flew by.

Oh great, I thought, that's just what I wanted to hear. I told Vandal that the only RPG's I saw were the ones fired at Doc when we first made contact with the convoy. I had no idea that so many RPG's were fired at us that day. He told me that they figure over 25 RPG's were fired at us that day.

Vandal told us how happy they all were as soon as we showed up, and wanted to just kick back and watch us pummel the Taliban, since he had a front row seat.

Another story that Vandal told us was about a senior ranking Taliban Mullah that had to be evacuated to a hospital in Peshawar Pakistan. Apparently, that mullah had pointed an RPG straight up in the air to try and shoot us as we flew over. Once he fired off the RPG, the back blast ricocheted off the ground all around him and caught his man dress on fire. Apparently, he was burned up pretty bad. We all laughed at that bit of good news. Vandal also told us that we killed about 48 insurgents, but the official count of those we killed was closer to 27, because the local Afghans do not like the Arabs, and don't count them amongst their dead.

Having started off my career in the infantry, on the ground, I could empathize with Vandal 1-6 and all the other soldiers on the ground in Afghanistan.

I remembered all the Vietnam vets I had talked to, and most everybody else that had seen any war movies, how they viewed helicopter pilots. Everyone seemed to have the same idea. That it was just the sound of the helicopter rotor blades in the distance coming in to help out whoever needed help. Inside each one of those helicopters were brave, Warrant Officers coming in to save them, no matter how bad the shooting was.

Just like in the days of the U.S. Cavalry, years ago.

I, for one, was very happy that October 4th came out the way that it did. This was just another reminder of why I was there in Afghanistan, in a helicopter, at this time in my life. I may have killed a few other human beings, but I did it to save American lives.

And for that I have no regrets whatsoever.

Group shot of Tagab valley convoy rescue crew.
One of the pilots is pointing at the bullet hole in the tail rotor driveshaft.

Safety belt around tailboom of QRF Apache,
as our mini rebellion to law.

Chapter 8

Unknown Battles

Lisa   *There were a couple of times while he was gone that we couldn't talk at all. If a couple of days went by with no contact, it was okay, but come the fourth day I would start to worry, and wonder why I hadn't heard from him. I would search the news to see if there was something I missed. The longer the time became, the more jumpy and irritable I became, and it was like living in a constant state of suspense. I would walk around with a million things on my mind and my kids could see on my face how stressed and worried I was. My son was too young to understand fully what I was going through, but he had a sense that something was wrong. If I was being quiet he would ask me if I had heard from Dad or if Dad was ok. My daughter would reassure me that he was ok. She had so much faith in her father, and she knew absolutely that he was okay. All three of us were going through the same thing in a different way, and we were all completely in tune with each other.*

Three quarters of the way through my deployment, I didn't know if it was the weight of my body armor or the weight of my experiences over the last year, but every day my neck and shoulders were throbbing and aching more and more. I was constantly trying to rub the pain out of my muscles. When I looked at some of the videos of myself flying I could tell I was in pain and uncomfortable as I was constantly readjusting all of the equipment I was wearing. I would shrug my shoulders in different directions to try and readjust all the weight that was hanging on them, which was close to 60 pounds worth of body armor and survival vest.

Fortunately, I finally had some relief from my anxiety/claustrophobia, but that was to be short-lived.

I had started contemplating how I would match the experience of being in combat and the adrenaline rush that I felt after being in a shoot out. I would catch myself saying a prayer or talking to God in my own way as I was pre-flighting my aircraft or preparing to enter a known Taliban stronghold. I was more and more complacent with being shot at or having an aircraft malfunction. Watching tracer rounds arc through the air toward my aircraft no longer excited me. I was more frustrated with the activities and the way of life on the airbase at Bagram.

Bagram airbase was getting busier and busier every day as more soldiers and civilians showed up. My patience was getting shorter and shorter at these Fobbit's that were multiplying like rabbits within the safe confines of the airbase.

Fobbit's was a term the Shooters used, referring to those that never left the safe confines of a Forward Operating Base (FOB) and there were plenty of jokes, all around, referring to them.

Fobbit's were definitely essential to the daily operations of war, though. After all, somebody had to order the toilet paper, food, and ammunition. Most of the noncombatants just did their jobs and minded their own business, never really associating with the infantry and aviation types that left the airbase as a part of their jobs. The really annoying Fobbit's were the ones that kept the military stores in business. These people were easily identifiable by their well-kept clean uniforms and store-bought medals and knives that would make Rambo jealous. The only thing these people used their knives for was to open their care packages full of Ding Dong's and HO HO's.

And then there was always the one that would cross the line.

One day, I flew a Fallen Hero mission. A Fallen Hero mission is a flight where an Apache would escort a medevac Blackhawk to some remote FOB to pick up an American soldier who was killed in combat. Once we returned to Bagram, the control tower would hold all flights until we were on the ground. Everyone knew a Fallen Hero mission was another American who was killed in combat in defense our country. The Blackhawk would taxi up to the main terminal and there would be a special detachment of soldiers waiting for the special cargo. The casket with the Fallen Hero would be placed in the back of a Humvee and driven slowly down the main boulevard to a building before being sent home. The BIG VOICE, which is what we called the PA system, would announce that a Fallen Hero was arriving and would be driven down "Disney Avenue", the main boulevard. Everyone on the base, that was able to, would line the streets on both sides and would stand at attention and salute as the procession slowly drove by. I guess it was God's way of slapping me back to reality, because this was the first Fallen Hero procession that I was ever able to attend. Normally I was busy shutting down the aircraft while the procession was happening or I was out flying around somewhere in the country, trying to prevent a fallen hero ceremony from ever happening in the first place.

As I stood alongside one of the female Chinook pilots from the 10th Mountain division, the procession drove slowly past us. I stood there at the position of attention, with the most perfect salute I could muster and silently said a prayer for the Fallen Hero and her family that would have no doubt heard the terrible news by now.

While alongside the other soldiers showing their last respects, I had a vision of my house. It seemed as if I was standing on my front porch as a government vehicle drove up and parked in front. As the doors closed shut, I looked to my left at my front door as it opened up and standing in the doorway was Lisa with Shelby and Eric on either side of her. Lisa had a look of despair and sadness as she watched the two uniformed officers make their way down the driveway to them. I could see Eric holding tightly to Lisa's waist as he was desperately trying to hold back his tears, not fully comprehending what the two uniformed men were coming to their house for. I then looked at Shelby as she was standing there with a smile on her face. She seemed at ease with knowing how this would turn out.

I then snapped back to the present time on the other side of the world. As the procession went by, everyone turned around and walked back to do the business that they were involved with before the Fallen Hero ceremony started.

I then thought about how every day I was away, Lisa, Shelby and Eric would say prayers for my safety, yet start each day wondering if this was the day that a government vehicle was to pay a visit with the unthinkable news.

I turned around and started walking back to my B-Hut, my home, I noticed a group of Air Force personnel standing to the side of the walkway talking. Normally I would have just walked on by, taken a quick glance at their rank and either render a salute to a higher ranking officer or return a salute from an enlisted soldier. In this case, a female airman turned around and had a look of astonishment as she eyed me. At first, I thought maybe my flight suit zipper was undone. She broke away from the group and made a beeline to block me. I stopped and had this look of puzzlement as to why she was staring at me like I was on fire.

She proceeded to tell me that I was wearing a completely unauthorized piece of headgear while on the base. Apparently, a Boonie hat (a Vietnam era style, floppy brimmed, camouflaged hat) was unauthorized while walking around on the airbase. For some unknown reason I decided to answer her, and told her I had just returned from a flight picking up a Fallen Hero, and that I was just now returning from the Fallen Hero ceremony. That did not faze her as she continued demanding that I must immediately take my Boonie hat off. I could tell that she was a Fobbit. If she would've been a guy, I would've punched her right there. I could feel the anger build up inside of me as she started ranting about uniforms, while being on the base. I don't even know what all she said, all I could hear was that Charlie Brown teachers gibberish, Waa Waa Wa Wa Wah Waa. I wanted to berate her in front of all her friends as to how dare she even think about talking to me! I wanted to tell her that all I want to hear from her was "A thank you" to me and all the other combatants that were outside the safety of this airbase fighting this war for her. How dare she even think about scolding someone wearing a hat that she didn't like, much less someone she didn't even know! I stepped off to the side and continued walking on. I could hear her in the background saying that she was going to report me to someone . . . yeah right.

Thank God, for my own safety, I left the next day to Jalalabad for my monthly rotation there. The good thing about Jalalabad was you were closer to the fighting in the Hindu Kush and further away from all the Fobbit's in Bagram.

At Jalalabad airfield (Jaf), the intelligence we were given was since fall had arrived, the snow would start coming down in the high country, and the Taliban would go away for the winter season. We started doing missions further and further north along the Pakistan border. 10th Mountain had made headway into the Kamdesh and Gowardesh valleys, which were lined with the highest mountains in Afghanistan, topping out at over 19,000 feet. I thought the Pech and Waygal valleys had some high mountains, they did not compare to the ones we were now flying around.

In the Gowardesh Valley we could see over the ridgeline to the east, which was the Pakistan border, and see the city of Chitral in far northern Pakistan. The valleys were much sheerer than what we had been flying amongst all year. Even the bottom of the valleys had less than 100 feet of flat space between the mountain peaks around them. Still, there was no way to land at the bottom of the valleys because the rivers were usually 90 feet wide and the other 10 feet were covered by trees.

In the Gowardesh Valley, I was flying an escort mission for two Chinooks who were to deliver two platoons worth of soldiers to the newest outpost, Stonewall. It was close to 8000 feet above sea level. The mission for the night was for me to dart ahead of the two Chinooks, then fly over the first intended Landing Zone (LZ) and make sure that it was okay for them to land there.

It was to be done at night and it is what our NVS (Flir system) was good at. We flew over the LZ, and I reported back to the Chinooks, which were inbound behind me, there looked to be tree stumps and a herd of small animals situated on the actual LZ. As I continued circling over the LZ I noticed a very small house with a campfire just outside its door and I informed them about this also. Apparently that didn't matter because one Chinook had already begun their approach to the LZ. The pilot said he was going to try to land there anyway and I watched in amazement as the Chinook hovered over the stump riddled LZ trying to decide whether to continue his landing or not. I then noticed what looked like small marshmallows rolling in different directions away from the Chinook and then I realized it was a herd of sheep that the Chinook's rotor wash was blowing across the small open field. I then noticed the campfire that was in front of the small cabin was also being blown around by the tremendous rotor wash. It would've been a funny sight to behold if this wasn't a war zone. The whole purpose of inserting the troops into this new outpost was the high mountain valley was actually a thoroughfare for the Taliban coming from Pakistan. The lead Chinook realized that the LZ would not work because the tree stumps were too high for them to get low enough for the troops to jump out safely. I flew about one kilometer to the South of the LZ to the second LZ that was in the operations plan, and it looked much better than the first one. I circled over it to make sure it was clear of any stumps or other things such as sheep and then I turned on our latest toy.

IZLID was a several thousand watt laser pointer that was attached to our 30 mm gun. It had a safety range of several miles. If we shined the laser at a person within a certain distance and they happened to be looking at it, they would be instantly and permanently blinded. It would actually cause physical burns within a few hundred meters, and needless to say, if used properly it was an added weapon attached to our aircraft. Another good thing about it, no one could see it with the naked eye. The only people who could see it were friendly troops who had night vision goggles.

So for the first time we turned on the IZLID. I had taken off my night vision system and switched over to night vision goggles so I could see what the laser actually looked like. The sight was unbelievable. Imagine a light saber 300 feet long and 2 inches thick. I swear I could almost hear the electronic sound reverberating just like in Star Wars as we moved the laser around pointing at the LZ.

The second LZ proved to be just fine. Both Chinooks successfully landed and delivered the two platoons of soldiers that were to occupy the new outpost. All three aircraft, the two Chinooks and I, said our goodbyes to the infantry soldiers that were now on the ground. I couldn't even imagine what it must have been like for those soldiers. They were at the most northern and remote outpost in Afghanistan, it was close to midnight, and the temperature outside hovered around freezing. There were no clouds in the sky, just the brilliant stars in the clear cold night. We completed that mission in under an hour.

Making our way south along the Konar River, we passed the northernmost base in the valley, Naray. We continued south towards Jalalabad, which was close to 50 miles away. I had my night vision goggles on and preferred to fly the rest of the flight this way as opposed to using the Flir system on the aircraft. Even with the thousands of hours I had flying with the NVS, it was still very tiring to concentrate with only your right eye to fly with. Besides, with the night vision goggles on I could see millions more stars than I ever could with just the naked eye and since Night Vision Goggles(NVG's) amplified light several thousand times, I could see falling stars, and muzzle flashes if anybody was shooting at us.

Flying along the valley, I noticed some flashes over the mountains to my right. I only had to wait a few more seconds before I saw more flashes and realized they were on the other side of the mountain. It puzzled me and I thought maybe there was a thunderstorm on the other side of the mountain. My copilot had also seen the flashes and asked me if I thought there was a storm approaching. I kept staring at the top the mountains and noticed a dark object moving around in the sky. It would periodically go behind the mountains, and then I would see it again a few seconds later. The next time I saw it, I noticed what looked like a short burst of laser light coming from it. Then a few seconds later it looked like there were lightning flashes just on the other side of the mountain top. I strained my eyes, concentrated as hard as I could through the night vision goggles, and tried to figure out what was going on. After watching another short burst of lines coming from the object in the sky, I realized it was an AC-130 Specter gunship. Somewhere on the other side of the ridgeline Special Forces were dealing death in the middle of the night. That's when I remembered a few days earlier, back at Bagram, I saw a Special Operations Chinook helicopter hovering with Rangers rappelling out of the tailgate. They were practicing for what was undoubtedly a "Snatch and Grab" mission of some high-value target that had been discovered living high up in the mountains.

Watching the AC-130 circling and shooting at some target on the ground reminded me of a Bible verse that said something like, *"in the end of times, there will be wars and rumors of wars".*

We made the rest of the trip back to Jalalabad without any further incidents. Just a few months left before I was finally to go home was all I could think as I laid my head down to sleep.

The next night I was on Quick Reactionary Force (QRF). Both crews, including myself, of the Apache QRF flight were in the main Tactical Operations Command (TOC) watching a bootleg copy of the series "24". The battle Captain, who is the person in charge of all flights coming and going out of Jalalabad, said it was going to be a slow night since there were no scheduled flights coming or going out. I wished he never would've said that because sure enough, 30 minutes later, we were called out on a QRF mission to the Korengal Valley. As always, it seemed just the mention of Korengal Valley was enough to get my anxiety level up.

Both Apache crews made our way out to the flight line and started spooling up our aircraft. I was to be chalk two, or trail aircraft on this flight. The standard plan was to depart north out of Jalalabad area, head up the Konar River Valley towards Asadabad, make a left turn and then head west for a few miles before turning south into the Korengal Valley itself. It was like flying a big upside down J getting to the actual Korengal Valley. This time, flight lead asked me if I wanted to just fly straight from Jalalabad, over the mountains, directly to the Korengal Valley. He was already headed straight for the mountains and I told him, "No, we better not".

There were several reasons I could think of as to why that might not be a good idea. One was climbing directly from where we were at and flying straight to the KOP would mean we would have to climb over 12,000 foot mountains, at night, over some extremely unforgiving terrain. Second, normally the fights in the Korengal Valley were in the southern end so making a direct flight would mean we would have no communications with anyone in the valley until we crested over the last ridgeline at the southern end. If there was a Fire Mission going on, we would end up flying straight into it, with no warning whatsoever of any incoming artillery rounds.

After starting our initial flight towards the mountains, we made a right turn to continue up the Konar River Valley. Normally, we follow the rules of the road, meaning we stayed on the right side of whatever the main feature was we were flying over. If we were crossing a saddle on a ridgeline we would stay to the right side, in case there was another flight coming from the opposite direction. That meant if we were following a river, we would stay on the right side in case another flight was headed in the opposite direction. That flight would be on the right side of the river from their perspective. This rule was basically standard operating procedures for anywhere in the world. Funny thing is it was the Americans who established which side of the road was the *right* side of the road.

I was letting my copilot fly as I was making sure we were headed up the correct river valley and I was also busy making sure the weapons were going to be ready by selecting the correct type of rocket we would shoot once the fighting started. We were still slightly on the left side of the river, which was close to 300 yards wide, as we headed north. Flight lead was definitely taking his time getting over to the right side of the river as we were flying along.

One of the weaknesses with the Night Vision System (NVS) is at certain times and atmospheric conditions, you really couldn't see, or at least make out definite objects no more than one or 2 miles away. This was one of those nights. The humidity was much higher, which attenuates the night vision systems ability to see long distances clearly. There were also times when you really couldn't make out anything against some backgrounds, such as city lights or highways with lots of vehicles.

With my copilot on the flight controls, I glanced down at my radio on the right panel to make sure the frequencies were correct before we entered the fight. Flight lead was about a hundred meters to our left front, my 10 o'clock position. We were both at the same altitude, barely 100 feet over the river.

One of the things you never want to hear your copilot say is, "Oh shit", especially when you are not expecting it. At that moment, my copilot yelled out "Oh shit!" I looked out the right side of my aircraft and saw the silhouette of a Blackhawk helicopter flying the opposite direction, at our same altitude, less than 25 meters away. I immediately looked straight ahead and saw another Blackhawk fly directly over us, also less than 25 meters away. Simultaneously, another Blackhawk flew between flight lead and our aircraft in the opposite direction.

I quickly told the copilot to turn in and get directly behind flight lead because I didn't know how many more aircraft were still headed southbound. At the same time, flight lead said there was a flight passing through us. Just like that, a flight of two Apaches and a flight of at least three Blackhawks had come within a hair's breath of having a catastrophic midair collision over the Konar River.

We continued our flight northbound with nobody saying anything. It was dead silent over the Common Air to Ground (CAG) frequency. I don't know if the Blackhawk flight ever saw us or not. It was the same thing in our flight, nobody said another word. I could not believe that we had come that close to dying.

A few miles later, as we passed FOB Asadabad, the radio came to life. The controller at the FOB said the fight was over in the Korengal and we were to return back to Jalalabad. We turned around and made the 30 minute flight back to Jalalabad with nobody saying another word.

Once back on the ground at Jalalabad, I went into the TOC and asked the battle Captain if he knew who the flight of Blackhawks was that we almost hit. He was as shocked as we were that anybody else was out there. He made a call back to Bagram to see if they knew who that flight was and Bagram also said they had no clue who that flight was and made an assumption that it was most likely a Special Operations flight, they never talk to anyone else.

I could only guess that it was the Rangers coming back from the fight a few nights earlier that I had seen.

The next day I was tasked on an escort mission with 2 Chinooks. This was to be a standard mission, like all the previous "ring route" missions I had been doing all year. On the runway at Jalalabad I watched as the 2 Chinooks took off to the east and then made a turn to the north. I took off about a minute behind them and made a straight line to catch up to them. The Chinooks were no more than a mile ahead of me when I passed the controls of my aircraft to my copilot. As soon as he had the controls, the aircraft made a quick left/right rolling motion. He quickly asked me if I had bumped the controls? I replied that no I had not touched the controls at all. I told him that maybe we had flown through the rotor wash of the Chinooks we were behind. I then took the controls back and sure enough, the aircraft made another quick left then right rolling motion. I maneuvered the Apache to a position I knew was not in the rotor wash of the Chinooks. Sure enough the rolling motion happened again but this time it continued.

The aircraft was doing its own left right rolling oscillations with no inputs from the pilots.

I recognized this from before. My accident, years earlier, was caused by an un-commanded flight control input. I quickly disengaged the flight control stabilization system with my thumb on a red button on the cyclic. Sure enough the oscillations stopped. I quickly called the Chinooks and told them that I had a problem with my aircraft and was returning to Jalalabad. With the Stabilization equipment disengaged the aircraft flew sluggishly and sloppy. I reengaged the unaffected "pitch" and "roll" channels and made an uneventful landing back at Jalalabad. Both my copilot and I jumped out of our aircraft and hopped into the spare aircraft and a few minutes later launched on the mission with the Chinooks, whom had returned and were waiting on their armed escort. No aircraft were allowed to operate in this country solo. No Chinooks and Blackhawks were allowed to operate in the eastern Area of Operations (AOR) without an armed escort, it was the law.

That little incident brought back vivid images and memories of my crash years earlier. I couldn't even imagine being in a fight and having this aircraft doing something I didn't want it to do.

Fallen Hero procession on Disney avenue, Bagram airbase.

Chapter 9

Jurassic Park

*Lisa   Our daughter had a picture of herself and Daniel from the father/
daughter dance they went to, hanging in her locker at school. The picture
got lost one day and she was inconsolable. She was crying at school and had
teachers helping her try to find it. She was freaked out because that was her
connection to her dad, and the loss of the picture felt like losing him. Our son
also had a picture of Daniel with him at school and his teacher made sure no
one bothered it and they always knew where it was.*

The weather in Afghanistan is just like back in the southeast Texas. In
the spring and summer the days started off nice and hot and by time the
afternoon rolled around, thunderstorms would fire up, especially over the
mountains of the Hindu Kush. The ongoing problem in Afghanistan was
there were no accurate/predictable weather forecasts, other than what the
locals would tell us, because there was no weather radar. The best thing the
Air Force weather personnel could do was give us their best guess for the
day's weather from whatever historical data they could come up with.

A problem flying in the high mountain valleys was weather building
up on the other side of one ridgeline and then a thunderstorm moving over
the ridgeline and into the valley you were flying in. Most of the valleys are
box canyons with extremely high mountains all around. If a thunderstorm
came up and blocked you in, it would be very dangerous, if not impossible,
to try to climb out through the clouds and over the high mountains. With
the mountains of the Hindu Kush rising well over 14,000 feet, it would
have been suicidal to try to fly up over one ridgeline and into an unknown
Valley on the other side, especially with clouds obscuring the tops of the
ridgelines or mountains.

When we had our first briefings coming into Afghanistan, what caught
my attention the most, were the two killers of pilots. One was the terrain
and the other was the weather. The chances of getting shot down were

rare. One of my fears was to be caught in a box canyon with ridgelines on all three sides too high to climb over and having a thunderstorm come up from the only escape route, blocking us in, and then squeezing us into the mountain walls.

The Taliban had made it well known how bad they wanted to knock an Apache out of the sky. There were numerous radio intercepts of Taliban commanders ordering their soldiers to commence or continue a fight, only to have their lieutenants tell them that they couldn't do anything because "Apaches were in the area" It was well known that to knock an Apache out of the sky would be great, but to actually capture an Apache pilot alive would be the greatest gift of all. We had all been made very aware of the consequences of getting knocked out of the sky and being taken alive by the Taliban. The outcome would have been death for us in the end, but what was most disturbing was the torture that a captured pilot would endure before finally being video-taped having their head cut off for the entire world to see, on Al Jazeera.

I was on my usual three week temporary reassignment to Jalalabad. The mornings started off with a prayer call sent out over loudspeakers around the Jalalabad airport. The air was thick and heavy with humidity as the heat built up. Usually after nine o'clock in the morning it was already too hot and too humid for any activity such as going to the gym, which was made of a bunch of broken equipment underneath a non-air-conditioned tent.

On that day both of us Apache crews were on quick reactionary force (QRF).

As an instructor pilot in our troop, I had to give instruction to several of the other pilots that were new to the Apache helicopter. I was paired up with Paul, and although Paul had thousands of hours flying in the Army, all those hours were in the CH 47 Chinook helicopter. When we pre-flighted our aircraft, I was in the front seat and Paul was in the back.

We called it the "five o'clock TIC" (troops in contact). It seemed that every day all was quiet until around five o'clock which was usually when we would receive a call to escort one of the medevac Blackhawks up to anyone of the remote valleys north of Jalalabad in the Hindu Kush.

Knowing that was a common occurrence, I made my way to the air-conditioned maintenance building, down by the flight line, at around three o'clock in the afternoon. During the day, the air-conditioned maintenance building was the best place to hang out. Berto, the pilot in command of the other QRF Apache, was also down there.

Our Captain was Berto's front seat copilot while we were in Jalalabad. Berto, like myself, had thousands of hours flying the Apache and we had been flying together since the mid-1990s. Berto's son was born the day I had my crash back in 1995.

Both the Captain and my copilot were very new to the Apache. Even though they were both pilots, they were still learning all the intricacies of the Apache itself, as opposed to the more senior aviators, who flying the Apache was second nature to. We could concentrate on supporting the ground units, or firing weapons, and not have to worry about the "monkey skills" of flying the aircraft. It was a complicated dance to coordinate who you were talking to and who needed what kind of help and where the good guys were and where the bad guys were, during a fight. Throw into the mix, high altitude flying in rugged mountainous terrain, people screaming into the radios during a fight, aircraft engines and transmissions being pushed to their upper limits and making sure you never have a friendly fire incident, were all the things a pilot had to think of and do without fail.

We were sitting under the porch outside the maintenance building and looked north towards the Hindu Kush mountains. I could see thunderstorm clouds starting to rise up in the distance. Judging by the front range mountains that were 14,000 feet or higher I could see some very dark, ominous clouds in some of the thunderstorms that were building up, which meant some very intense thunderstorms were in store for the rest of the day.

Just like clockwork, right around five o'clock, our QRF radio crackled to life. It was the battle captain at the tactical operations command (TOC) advising us of a pending medevac mission. He told us to start heading towards our aircraft. Since Berto and I were already at the flight line, we started the auxiliary power units (APU) for our respective aircraft. We also started the alignment of the navigation system, but mainly getting the air conditioner going to start cooling off the aircraft was the real reason we started the APU. Within a few minutes we could see the Gator (ATV) bringing the medevac Black Hawk crew to their aircraft. A moment later, both Paul and the Captain came running around the HESCO barriers towards our aircraft. Within moments all three aircraft were at 100% RPMs and listening intently to the radios. Once all three aircraft checked in as being ready to take off, the TOC called and told us the location of the mission.

As usual, this medevac mission would be going into the Korengal Valley.

With the aircraft ready to launch, we contacted the tower at Jalalabad and got clearance to take off to the North. Berto and I had been flying together for years, so we just naturally keyed off of each other to cover the Blackhawk helicopter leading the way up the Konar River. In route up the Konar River valley towards Asadabad, we were contacted on the radio and told that the fight was still going on in the Korengal Valley. We decided to leave the Blackhawk at FOB (forward operating base) Asadabad because having two Apaches shooting it out with the Taliban, while maintaining separation between us was a lot to think about. It was just too risky to have the medevac Blackhawk flying around in the valley while there was shooting going on.

The plan was for the two Apaches to help the infantry soldiers in the fight and once the fighting was over and it was safe for the Blackhawk to come into the valley, we would head back to FOB Asadabad, refuel and rearm, if needed, and then return with the medevac Blackhawk to pick up the wounded soldier.

As we flew northbound on the east side of FOB Asadabad, we saw the Blackhawk peel off of our formation and begin his landing approach to the FOB. We continued northbound.

About 2 miles north of FOB Asadabad is the actual city of Asadabad. I was in the lead, and as we passed the city we made a left turn westbound up the Pech River Valley towards the Korengal Valley, which was a few miles ahead. I told Paul, who was in the backseat and flying the aircraft, what we might see and expect as we approached the fight.

Seven miles later we made our left turn southbound into the Korengal Valley and all of the radios burst to life. Everyone seemed to be calling for help and making corrections to the mortar teams as they were frantically shooting high explosive rounds in support of the patrol that was in the fight. Looking at the navigation system I could see that the troops in contact were south of the Korengal outpost (KOP). As I looked south over the KOP, I could see the smoke of the actual fight we were going to support. It was at this point that I quickly realized that our flight path was going to take us directly over the KOP.

I looked just ahead and noticed peculiar smoke coming up from the KOP. At first I couldn't tell what the smoke was and then I saw it. The KOP was in the middle of a fire mission with their mortars! All of the radios were screaming with activity and it was total chaos. To make things worse, somebody out there was running the IED jammers over the radio systems which would send out a high-pitched, loud, shrill noise over most of the frequencies we were using to communicate with. It is virtually impossible to communicate with the radio that is being jammed and you couldn't just turn off the radio or turn the volume all the way down, because if the unit that was jamming stopped, there was no way to know when someone was trying to contact you.

Paul had taken over the controls and was in charge of flying the aircraft. As an instructor pilot, I allowed Paul to control the aircraft and what and where we shot. I would just handle the radios and give Paul corrections or guidance as needed.

Over the intercom system I told Paul that I had not established communications with the KOP and for him NOT to continue over the KOP, as mortars were being fired directly through our intended flight path. All the radios were screaming at us so much that Paul either didn't hear me over the intercom communication system (ICS), or couldn't understand what I had told him. As we continued flying closer to the KOP, I saw the mortar crews dropping fresh rounds into the tubes and the flames come out with the high explosive shell arcing up straight through the altitude and flight path we were flying in.

I started screaming over the ICS for Paul to make a left turn so we wouldn't get hit by an outbound mortar round, at the same time I was reaching up with my hands and pointing to the left, hoping that he would see my hands in front of his face, over the roar of all the radio traffic.

Paul finally responded to me as he started turning the aircraft and asked me what was so urgent. I screamed back at him asking if he had seen the mortars being fired from the KOP directly through our intended flight path.

He apparently didn't realize how close we had come to getting hit by our own troops on the ground. He was silent for a few minutes, probably thinking about what I had just said and finally realizing how close we came to getting knocked out of the sky by our own soldiers.

I found out later from Berto that he was also wondering if we were going to fly directly over that outbound mortar fire. He was right on the edge of giving us a call, but he was also overwhelmed and drowned out by all the radio traffic and Warlock (the IED jammer).

I finally made contact with the KOP fire controller and he cleared us south, over the KOP, towards our troops that were still being fired upon by the Taliban.

Once overhead, I made contact with the ground troops that had the wounded soldier and were still being engaged by the Taliban. The ground commander told us that possibly three enemy soldiers were on a ridgeline leading up the Abaskar Ridge. I told Paul to start making turns to set up and shoot up the ridge, where the enemy soldiers were most likely hiding.

I didn't have to tell Berto what we were about to do since he was just following my lead, and I was doing my best to let Paul set up for the attack runs on his own and just give him some advice as needed.

This valley is primarily a north-south valley. The Abaskar ridge is at the south end of the Korengal Valley and has small ravines leading down both sides of the ridgeline. Paul originally set up on a north-south attack run shooting across the tops of the ravines. I kept telling him that if I were an enemy soldier trying to hide from the Apaches, I would most likely hide down in the bottom of the ravines. He continued his north-south attack runs for a few more turns and each time shooting rockets across the top of the gullies coming down from the Abaskar ridge. Each time after Paul would fire rockets, I would shoot the gun down into the bottom of the ravines where I thought the Taliban would be hiding. I would also remind him, over and over again, that the Taliban were most likely hiding out at the bottom of the ravines that we were shooting across.

On the north to south attack runs the sun was shining right in our faces. In desperation I finally told Paul to try altering his race track pattern from north-south to east-west *into* the gullies. He finally agreed and altered his attack runs to start coming more from the east to the west, into the face of the Abaskar Ridge. We were still facing the sun on our inbound runs, but at least it was more from the left front instead of straight into our faces. As we were making our outbound turn from an attack run, Paul saw the three Taliban soldiers about midway up the ridge. The Taliban soldiers made a fatal mistake, they moved. As soon as they made any kind of movement we could easily pick them out.

The Taliban, having lived their entire lives in these high-altitude mountains, had no problem climbing up the mountains, as opposed to taking the easy route going down. The locals were acclimated to this high rugged mountainous country and could easily outrun our fittest Special Forces soldiers, without so much as a few beat increase in their heart rates.

I called Berto and told him we had seen three Taliban soldiers about halfway up the mountain and to keep an eye on where our rockets impacted on our next attack run so he could gauge off of that on his next run.

It was at this point we noticed the sun was no longer glaring in our faces because a thunderstorm had been forming on the valley west of the Korengal, and had been moving east over the ridgeline quickly towards us.

We made several runs shooting rockets and bullets at the last position where we had seen the Taliban soldiers. I don't know if we killed those guys, but if they lived through the onslaught of two Apaches shooting rockets and high explosive bullets all in that area, then they deserved to live.

We were low on gas and ammunition at this point and decided to return to Asadabad to refuel. I called up the ground controller for the platoon that was taking fire and had the wounded soldier and told him we were headed back to FOB Asadabad to pick up the medevac helicopter, refuel, and rearm ourselves. As we left northbound out of the Korengal Valley, we saw huge thunderstorms building up to the West. I discussed with Berto the possibility that we may not be able to make it back to the Korengal due to the weather building up and moving to the east. He agreed with me but said that we should, at the very least, give it our best shot to get the wounded soldier out.

Over the city of Asadabad we made contact with the Blackhawk and told him of the weather building up to the west. The medevac had been sitting on the ground at FOB Asadabad, was full of fuel and ready to go at a moments notice. Berto and I had to get more fuel and rearm before we could go back into the Valley.

Our final approach to the FOB had both Apaches lined up one behind the other so we could land adjacent to the fuel line. Since I landed in front of Berto, the ground crews decided to rearm me first while Berto was refueled. This was standard procedure since there usually were not enough personnel to refuel and rearm multiple helicopters anyway.

After I was re-armed, I looked up to the right at the mountain bordering the west side of the FOB. There were ominous black storm clouds rolling over the top of the mountain and coming down towards the FOB. I expected the crew to start the refueling process for my aircraft at any moment. I was a surprised when Berto said he was ready to take off because he was fully armed and refueled. I quickly checked out my right window and asked Paul to make sure that we were not hooked up to the refuel line. It is extremely dangerous to transmit over the radio with a fuel line hooked up to the aircraft. Even though the aircraft was grounded, our radios could easily trigger a spark and cause an explosion of jet fuel if we made any radio transmissions during the refueling process.

I asked Paul if they had already refueled us since he was in the back seat, and closer to the refuel panel, he could see this more easily than I could. Paul told me, "No, nobody had come and attached the refuel line to the aircraft yet".

I call back to Berto and told him that apparently we were not getting refueled at this time because of the storm being so close. Now there were lightning strikes and droplets of rain started to fall around the FOB. Berto called back and said that's what he figured as well. The medevac Blackhawk chimed in with a call saying that they were ready to leave at this time, and all they needed was one Apache anyway. Berto and the Blackhawk took off to the north with the thunderstorm rolling in over the mountain on the west side of the FOB. Paul and I were stuck in the helicopter fully armed, but with no gas to take us anywhere. I signaled out my window for one of the refuel guys to come over to my aircraft and asked him why they were not refueling us. He confirmed what Berto and I had talked about; the lighting was too close and too frequent to safely refuel our aircraft.

Berto told me later that they didn't think they could make it to the previous area where we were shooting, because the thunderstorm was all over the Korengal Valley at that time. The medevac Blackhawk continued on and made it to the previous battle site, with Berto circling closely around them, meanwhile, thunderstorms were building up all around them. The medevac Blackhawk could not land in the area, so they had to winch up the wounded soldier with lightning striking all around.

Back at FOB Asadabad, I finally got the fuel that I needed and was still at 100% RPM so I could take off as soon as Berto and the medevac came back. It was now raining steadily on the FOB. Paul and I discussed that when the other two aircraft made it back from the Korengal valley, we would be in the air on the south side of the FOB, ready to continue the flight back to Jalalabad. We contacted the Asadabad controller, and told him that we were going to take off and circle about a mile south of the FOB. We would wait for the medevac and the other Apache to link up with us. Then all three of us would continue south to Jalalabad together.

As we circled about a mile south of the FOB, the storm grew increasingly larger to the north and was moving slowly south towards us.

The Pech River Valley, where Berto and the medevac Blackhawk were coming out of, was black as night from the rain and lightning. I was growing concerned with the situation at hand. It looked to me like they were blocked off from coming back out of the Pech river valley to Asadabad. The actual entrance to the Pech River Valley was being inundated with multiple lightning strikes and an absolute black wall of water. The ridgeline to the west was completely obscured now by the storm rolling in over the top. As we circled, waiting for the other two aircraft to join up with us, I looked to the south, where we had to go 25 miles to make it back to Jalalabad. I contemplated whether to try to beat the storm and make it to Jalalabad, to continue making circles here, or possibly land back at Asadabad.

I was thinking that Berto and the medevac could either land at the Korengal outpost or maybe go back even further west to camp Blessing to wait out the storm.

The decision whether or not to go back to FOB Asadabad and land was made for me in the next few seconds. As Paul and I were watching the storm coming south towards us, there were multiple lightning strikes on the landing zone (LZ) and the actual FOB was disappearing from view as a wall of water engulfed it. The south was our only escape route now but the storm was starting to spread from the ridgeline on the west and beginning to cut off this exit.

The valley is only a mile or two wide at its widest point and the mountains to the east of the valley border Pakistan. The storm coming from the north kept pushing us further and further south away from FOB Asadabad. It was becoming clear that we needed to make a beeline for Jalalabad as fast as we could fly because if the storm to our south crossed the valley to the east, we would be stuck in the valley with no friendly places to land.

I was worried about Berto and the Blackhawk, and whether they were safe on the ground at the KOP, or better yet, out of the Korengal Valley and safe on the ground at camp Blessing.

I radioed FOB Asadabad and asked what the conditions were on the LZ and if they had any information on the other two aircraft. FOB Asadabad radioed back saying that they could not even see the LZ because of the severe rain, and there was lightning striking all around them. The controller also said that they had no information on the medevac or its Apache escort.

Well, this pretty much confirmed that I was not able to go back to that LZ!

Just like in the movies, when all seemed lost, the radio crackled to life. The first transmission was totally indecipherable, but I could tell it was Berto.

I immediately pressed the push to talk switch and called back to Berto telling him where I was. He called back saying that they had just come out of the Pech River Valley, dropped off the wounded soldier, and were making their way along the river southbound towards me. They had to fly really low and slow to maintain visual contact with the river they were following. The sky above us was completely covered in clouds and the sun had already set to the west of the mountains, so the available sunlight was depleting quickly.

Berto told me later that they also didn't think they would make it out of the Pech River Valley, due to the tremendous amount of rain and lightning strikes around them. Both aircraft descended down to well below 100 feet above the ground, and basically hover taxied out of the Pech river valley because the visibility was so bad from the rain. They made a quick stop at the LZ at FOB Asadabad, dropped off the wounded soldier, and took off again to link up with us. It took less than one minute on the ground, in the middle of a torrential storm.

We had been doing circles over the Konar River, waiting for the other two aircraft, but were drifting slowly south away from the storm coming down from the north.

I radioed Berto to tell him that we were about 100 feet over the river and about 4 miles south of FOB Asadabad and I asked him if he could see us. I could not see the two aircraft coming south somewhere in the vicinity of FOB Asadabad. I asked Berto again, thinking they were closer, if they could see me now. He responded again telling me that they were out of the rain but still could not see us. The storm to our south was now nearly across the valley and almost touching the mountains to the east. Our escape route back to Jalalabad was getting dangerously closer and closer to being completely cut off. I told Paul to turn on our white anti-collision lights for a few seconds in hopes that Berto and the Blackhawk would see us. I then radioed again and asked if they could see our white strobes over the river. They again replied that they still could not see us.

I reached down on the cyclic and pressed the manual flare release button which fired off a salvo of flares. I then called Berto back and asked him if he could see the flares and he radioed that they now had a visual on me. I told him to catch up to me as fast as they could and maybe we could

138

skirt the eastside of the valley and get around the storm before we were totally blocked off.

Meanwhile, on the ground on the east side of the Konar River near my present position, was a Special Forces "A" camp. Several Special Forces soldiers stepped outside when they heard my Apache circling right out their front door and were all wondering why I was making circles over the river when a storm was approaching from the west. Then they saw me turn on my lights and fire off a salvo of flares. They all figured something was about to happen and had started gathering up the Afghan national soldiers and their weapons for a possible fight. Then they saw another Apache coming from the north following behind a Blackhawk link up with me and fly to the south at a high rate of speed.

It was becoming more apparent that we were going to have to climb up the ridgeline to our east to try and stay out of the storm, but the storms were building up so rapidly that even that option was closing off as fast as I could think about it. I radioed Berto and the Blackhawk to see how they felt about making a beeline east over the ridgeline into Pakistani airspace, then flying south towards Jalalabad. They agreed so we started climbing and turning more towards the mountains bordering Pakistan but it only took a few more seconds to realize that there was another storm on the east side of the ridgeline which blocked that route.

We were now officially closed off from flying south, or even east into Pakistan, to our home base of Jalalabad. Knowing that our route back to Asadabad was also closed off, we were officially up a river with no paddle and my worst nightmare was unfolding before my very eyes.

The only good thing about this nightmare was the valley we were in actually had flat places to land if we needed to. But even with that thought, I had to remind myself that there were so many land mines in this country that we had little chance of making a successful landing anywhere, other than a secure FOB.

At this worst moment and time, I suddenly remembered the location of the Special Forces A camp, Sarconi. I told Paul to make a 180° turn back towards Asadabad and simultaneously radioed the other two aircraft following us and told them about the camp. What I didn't tell them was the fact that I had never landed there before and I had only flown over it once. Again, I told Paul and the other two aircraft we needed to go as fast as we could. The storms were still coming in from the north and west, and I was afraid that we would be cut off from this last and seemingly only hope.

We began heading northbound from where we had just left at a high rate of airspeed, but just as we were starting to pick up our speed, I noticed Paul was starting to slow down again. At first I thought he knew something I didn't know, or could see something I could not see, so I didn't say anything. The storm was racing southbound from the north and from the west towards us. The clouds were turning a deep dark green with lightning flashing out of them. I then asked Paul why he was slowing down. He said the camp was directly in front of us only a mile away, so he was slowing down to land. I quickly shouted back, "No! It is still several more miles in front of us and if we don't get there as fast as possible, we won't beat the storm!" it was now starting to rain on us.

There were several small ridgelines coming in from the east, and Paul had mistakenly identified the first one as the ridgeline that the camp was on. It was now raining hard on us. One bad design about the Apache is that the visibility is poor when looking out the front of the back seat's canopy during a rain storm. Being an instructor pilot and being in the front seat on this flight, I already had my night vision goggles mounted on my helmet. I also had my FLIR cooled down and ready for use with the flick of a switch. Plus, being in the front seat, I only had to look out through one windshield, as opposed to being in the backseat, and having to look through a blast shield and an outside canopy.

As we were making our way north to the LZ, the rain was starting to come down with a vengeance. Paul was starting to line up on the Landing Zone, but since he had never been there, he was not quite sure where it was located at the camp. Still in instructor mode, I was allowing Paul to fly as much as possible without my input. But as we were getting closer to the LZ, the rain was getting heavier and heavier, and the visibility was getting worse and worse. I knew I would have to start telling Paul to make corrections on his flight path towards the LZ.

This LZ was very small. I had seen it used once before by a Chinook dropping off some supplies but that was in the daytime and in clear weather. I had flown cover for that Chinook and circled the camp while he made the landing, so officially, I had never actually landed there, and that mission had taken place several months earlier. I really wasn't sure if the LZ was still even there and worse yet, I really wasn't even sure if there were any Americans at that camp at all. I was leaving it all to luck that there were Americans there, and if not Americans, at least English-speaking/American friendly Afghan forces. I hoped they would protect us and not rejoice in the fact that two Apaches and a Blackhawk helicopter had just surrendered themselves to them.

As we were making our final approach to the LZ, I started giving Paul corrections to make sure we didn't hit the trees that were surrounding it. But now it was dark and the rain was coming down heavily. Paul did not have his night vision goggles on or his FLIR turned on. Then he started his descent too early, we were headed straight for the trees and the Hesco barriers that surrounded the camp and the landing zone.

Once again, although this time without the radios and IED jammers blasting in our ears, it seemed, Paul either couldn't hear me, or chose not to hear me. We kept on descending, headed straight for the trees and barriers. I again told Paul to stop descending, and to start turning to the right to line up for the LZ. He finally told me that he couldn't see out the front canopy because of all the rain and for me to take the controls of the aircraft and to fly us into the LZ.

Knowing that the other two aircraft behind me did not know anything about this LZ, I had to land as far forward as possible to give them room to land behind me, and as quickly as possible, before the rain and wind pushed them into the ground and before we couldn't see anything at all. As I was making my final corrections to land in the LZ, I knew it was going to be really tight. I had roughly 10 feet of clearance on both sides of my rotor system and a berm directly in front of me. I slammed the aircraft to the ground but kept my power on so I could roll as far forward as possible. I then jammed on the brakes to keep from hitting the berm in front of me and hoped I had given the other two aircraft enough room as possible to land safely in this tight LZ. As soon as I came to a stop, I lowered the collective and set the emergency brake. I had Paul turn on the searchlight and all the other lights on our aircraft. Hopefully the two other aircraft would have no problems seeing where we were, and therefore not land on top of us.

I then contemplated turning on the override switch. This would allow us to arm up and have control of the gun while on the ground; in case the Taliban came charging over the berm to attack us. That is one way we can shoot the gun while being on the ground.

I radioed the other two aircraft to see if they were on the ground safely behind me, and thank God they both responded with a "safe on deck" call. The rain seemed to acknowledge that we were all safe on the ground and commenced to come down in buckets for the next 10 minutes. I told Berto and the Blackhawk that we would at least try to cover the front of the LZ with our gun, if they would agree to cover our sides and behind us, as much as possible.

After about 10 minutes of this heavy downpour, the rain just stopped. Berto called me on the radio and gave me great news; American Special forces were at his aircraft and were surrounding the LZ to provide security for us.

Paul and I shut down our aircraft and I jumped out onto the muddy Afghan soil. Paul was excitedly telling me that he was "happy as could be" that we were on the ground safely.

I had hopped out with my video camera filming, trying to document as much of this as I could. As I looked back from the front of the aircraft towards the back, I couldn't believe my eyes. There was literally a big green wall of water coming at us. I yelled at Paul to close his canopy because we were going to get very wet. I scrambled back into the front seat of the Apache as fast as I could. The sky above had a bright green glow to the clouds that were boiling above us. Lightning was flashing through the clouds with no sounds of thunder there was an eerie calm around us.

All was quiet, too quiet.

Then the rain came down with a force like I had never seen in my entire life. The green glowing sky, the rain pouring down, and the lightning flashing all around reminded me of a scene in the movie Jurassic Park. The only thing missing, or should I say the only thing I was waiting for, was for some dinosaur to come brushing up against my canopy. The aircraft started shaking from side to side from the wind that was blowing all around us. We could hear the wind outside and knew it was strong because it was shaking 17,000 pounds worth of aircraft like it was a toy.

As I sat in the aircraft watching the rain and lightning all around us, I started to feel droplets of water trickling down my back and arms. The Apache's canopy is well known for leaking. The storm lasted for better than 15 minutes totally inundating the area.

As the storm moved on to the east, the sky was still lighting up with that eerie green glow emanating from the clouds every time there was lightning. The torrential downpour faded off to a light sprinkle but the visibility was still no more than about 100 meters all around, a ground fog had formed all around us.

I asked Paul if he thought the storm was over. He just let out a nervous laugh as he answered as far as he could tell, it was over. We both opened the canopies to our respective cockpits and climbed out of our aircraft onto the muddy ground again. Not knowing if the Special Forces and the Afghan national Army guys were still securing us, I stepped over the side of my aircraft to look back at the two aircraft that had landed behind us. Sure enough, the Blackhawk medevac crew, Berto and the Captain all started coming out of their aircraft at the same time. Slowly out of the mist, the Special Forces guys walked up to us.

We were all nervously talking about the close call we just had with the torrential storm almost making us land someplace we didn't want to. The Special Forces guys asked us if we wanted to come into their command center and wait out the remainder of the storm. With a resounding "yes" from all of us, we all started to follow the Special Forces soldiers back through the darkness towards their command post.

As we were walking, the Special Operations Forces (SOF) guys were asking us why we were circling just west of their FOB, turning our lights on and off and shooting flares, and why we then headed south, and then returned right as the storm hit.

As I was telling them what had transpired, I noticed something was nipping at my hand as I was walking. I looked down to see a dog following me on my right side, wagging his tail and occasionally jumping up to nip at my hand. I had not seen my own dog in almost a year, so I reached down to pet the dog, which was obviously very receptive at somebody showing some compassion towards him. We kept walking, and as I was trying to pet the dog he kept running ahead of me, stopping, looking around, and then waiting for us to catch up. He would then lick my hand and repeat the process over and over.

One of the SOFs guys commented that the dog confirmed I was an American soldier (as if we already didn't know). I kind of chuckled and asked him why he said that. He told me they kept the dogs on the FOB because the dogs didn't like the Taliban either, and were very faithful at alerting them whenever the Taliban was nearby.

The SOF guys finally led us to their command post and opened the door to let us in. What I saw next was actually what I envisioned seeing at any Special Forces A camp. There were old, but comfortable sofas and chairs in the main room and a nice TV hooked up to a satellite dish. On the walls were numerous weapons they had captured from the Taliban and Al Qaeda on all their missions. The weapons ranged from modern-day AK-47s to rifles that were just a few years newer than black powder muskets.

I walked around inside the small building admiring their collection in the main room and ended up in their mission planning room they had in back. I was looking at their maps, which they had laid out for their own mission planning purposes. One of the main maps, which caught my attention immediately, was a very detailed map of the Korengal Valley area. I started looking with special interest at the map, which showed all of their engagements, and certain villages and caves they had marked. I looked towards the south end of the Korengal Valley and one note leapt out at me.

On the southeast saddle of the Korengal Valley (on this map) was a note stating, "This was the last known whereabouts of Ahmad Shah"; I was flabbergasted because this was the exact location of the ambush that had shot up the Chinook, and fired the RPG at my aircraft just a few months earlier. This confirmed my suspicions as to why there were so many Taliban soldiers fighting so ferociously on the side of the mountain in that location. I figured it was Ahmad Shah's security force protecting him and we had just stumbled across them by accident. Right then thoughts raced through my mind as to maybe how close I had come to actually hitting Ahmad Shah.

The local SOF hosts offered us some food that they had left over from their evening's meal and that's when I realized how long I had been out shooting, flying, and now waiting out thunderstorms. I assumed they would offer us some MRE's or some other super special Green Beret meal, but what we got was some of the best food we had eaten the entire year we'd been in country. I don't know if it was because I was so hungry, or I was so tired, but that food was great.

The meal was Meat Loaf and mashed potatoes with vegetables that would make my mom's cooking pale in comparison.

While the medevac captain called on the landline back to Jalalabad, to let them know that we were all okay, the rest of us talked about the local events that were happening.

It took about two hours for all the thunderstorms in the area to dissipate and the ground fog to clear out then it was time to get back to our aircraft and head south to our own base, Jalalabad. Stepping out of the building, where there was electricity and lights, into the Afghan night was interesting. We could see well off in the distance some of the thunderstorms that were still spewing out lightning, however straight above us, the sky was perfectly clear after being washed clean by all the storms. It was one of those nights that without any moonlight, you could see the ground, just from the immense starlight overhead.

As soon as I had stepped out of the building, the same dog was sitting there playing by the front door. As if I was his master, he got up right next to me and started walking with me back to the aircraft. When we got up to the edge of the razor wire that covered the berm, which separated the base from our emergency landing area, one of the Special Forces sergeants commanded the dog to stop and wait there. The rest of us continued on to our respective aircraft. We made a quick preflight and then thanked every one of those Special Forces soldiers for their hospitality and great food. Most of all, we thanked them for being there when we needed them most. I told them that as we were making our final approach to the LZ, I was happy as could be that it was them, and not a bunch of Taliban soldiers that greeted us with open arms.

The only people that laughed at that comment were me and the Special Forces soldiers. I think that's when the other pilots realized I really didn't know what we were in store for when we landed there during that storm.

The flight back to Jalalabad, took only 20 minutes. It was a great feeling coming over the last ridgeline from the north and seeing the lights of the city of Jalalabad. What was even more comforting was having an American voice clear us to land at our airport in Jalalabad.

It was now close to midnight when we rolled into our own hooch's. I thought about going over to the computer tent to try and either call my wife and kids or at least instant message them. Midnight in Afghanistan was about the same time that my kids were awake and getting ready to go to school, so I figured I could at least try to talk to them before they left and started their normal daily routines back home.

I worked my way around the maze of tents in the dark towards the computer tent. As I rounded the last one I saw a line of people outside the tent waiting their turn. I turned around, headed back to my own hooch, and let out a sigh, knowing I would not be able to communicate with my family after all that had just happened today.

I got myself cleaned up and laid down in my bed. I slowly dozed off trying to visualize the routine that was happening at home. I was on the other side of the world and I had less than six months left before I went home for good.

God help me.

Jalalabad airport Quick Reactionary Force Apaches on standby for launch.
The Hindu Kush mountains are in the background,
with storm clouds building up.

Chapter 10

Something's Wrong

Lisa *At Christmas we wanted Daniel to be on the webcam while the whole family was there, but the satellite was down, which was extremely disappointing for everyone. The kids and I got to talk to him on Christmas Eve night, which was Christmas day for him. We got to watch him open the gift we sent him, on the webcam. It was a happy moment, and we were glad that our gift had made it to him, but it wasn't even close to being together for the holiday.*

After several days of not flying, due to a snowstorm, we were ready to get back in the saddle again. Allen and I were assigned to the quick reactionary force (QRF), which was good news, since we pretty much knew what our day was going to be like. Wake up at 0-dark thirty, get weather and mission brief, preflight the aircraft, get something to eat, then kick back the rest of the day and wait for a mission.

At the mission brief, I found out the other missions for that day were all resupply missions to the different FOB's throughout eastern Afghanistan. This was our area of responsibility, but one mission was different. There was a flight to the Korengal outpost, aka "The KOP", which was originally called the "Lumberyard". It was a little unnerving because that was where 90% of all our shootings had occurred throughout my tour. I was slightly relieved I wasn't on that mission because, I had just a few weeks left before I went home, and I didn't want to push my luck so close to the end.

After the generic portion of the daily brief was completed, Allen and I set out to preflight our aircraft and get something to eat. As I was leaving the briefing room the captain on the KOP mission told me if their aircraft (Apache) breaks they will jump in our Apache and go on the mission. This was standard operating procedure since their mission had priority and we didn't expect any QRF missions for a while. If their aircraft broke on run-up, our aircraft would be up on the auxiliary power unit (APU) and all we'd have to do is grab our stuff, jump out, and give it to the other crew to take immediately.

I would later regret not sticking around to hear the actual brief on their mission.

Allen and I pre-flighted then ran-up the aircraft to check the systems and radios for a possible QRF launch later that day. As we were sitting in the aircraft, letting the systems warm up, I noticed our captain running up to my cockpit. I told Allen "Get ready, It looks like we are about to give our aircraft to the other crew". I opened my canopy and the captain yelled out that his helmet is broken and we have to take the mission instead.

Each one of our helmets is fitted individually so you can't just take one helmet off of one person and use it on someone else. Also, the helmets cost over $15,000 each, so we don't keep extras lying around.

The captain handed me the mission packet with the frequencies, the route, and any pertinent information for the mission. The main flight consisted of 2 Blackhawk helicopters and one Apache as the armed escort. The concept of the mission was to escort one of the Blackhawks to the KOP, drop off a package, and get back without getting shot. I thought it was pretty straight forward, but I wasn't in on the original mission brief, so I really didn't know all the particulars. I started to get an uneasy feeling in the pit of my stomach.

We lined up on the taxiway and checked in with the entire flight as I was trying to convince myself that this should be an easy mission.

We launched east bound and passed by a canyon just east of Bagram where we completed a test fire of our gun to make sure it worked. Almost all the fights in the Korengal valley started with the gun and finished with rockets. Our gun's ability to move with our head and shoot where we were looking was what made it a must have for the Korengal valley fight, which is essentially a knife fight.

As we headed up the Konar river valley, north of Jalalabad, towards Asadabad, we were alerted on the radio there was a troops in contact (TIC) in progress in the Pech river valley. We were told to land at FOB Asadabad until the TIC was finished, because our route to the Korengal passed over that area. As we landed, I again got that really bad feeling in the pit of my stomach, like something was not right with the world. I also found out that a General was in the lead Blackhawk, and we were to drop him off at the KOP, along with "the package", and then return several hours later to pick him up. The General was to pay a visit to the troops that were based in the Korengal valley.

After we landed at Asadabad, the General got out of the Blackhawk and went into the tactical operations control center (TOC). Several minutes later, we got a call on the radio asking if we would like to go to the TIC sight, and help the ground troops finish it up. I called back and let them know that we were the only Apache there, and were not allowed to go "single ship" anywhere in-country.

A moment later we were given the coordinates of the actual TIC area which Allen input into the navigation computer. We found out the TIC was only 7 miles up the Pech river valley from the FOB. Allen and I discussed the scenario offered to us. I told him that this TIC is on the main route near a U.S. Patrol base, and if anything happens I feel confident we could make it to the patrol base safely. The General told the sergeant on the radio to let him know that *He* was authorizing us to go single ship. Allen and I discussed the situation further and agreed. We told the TOC that we could do this. Shortly thereafter, we were given permission to leave the FOB and proceed to the TIC sight, single ship.

In route to the TIC, Allen and I discussed what we were going to do once we got in contact with Dog 37, which was the ground unit involved with the TIC. As we approached the location, we attempted several times to establish contact with Dog 37. They eventually responded back to let us know they were attacked by several insurgents with RPG's from the ridgeline on the south side of the main valley. We told them we would look in the area where the RPG attacks came from. At first look, I started thinking the insurgents were gone, and we wouldn't find any sign of them. Also, in the back of my mind, I was thinking about being out there single ship, which was definitely not standard operating procedure. After a few minutes of searching for any sign of movement, I called Dog 37 and asked them if they had any friendly troops in the immediate search area because we wanted to fire off a "Willy Pee" (white phosphorous rocket) so they could adjust fire for us from the impact point. Dog 37 confirmed there were no friendly troops in the area, so I set up an attack run for a point that I would expect someone to be hiding. I fired off one White Phosphorous rocket and it hit the ridgeline near the entrance to the Shuriyak Valley, which is a known Taliban hide out. I called Dog 37 and asked them to tell us where the attack came from referenced to the rocket impact. They said the insurgents were most likely in the area where the rocket impacted, and possibly behind the ridgeline from there.

We made maneuvers to line the Apache up to fire more rockets and 30 mm bullets at the ridgeline, in what is referred to as "Recon by Fire". We were doing our best to find any kind of human movement that would indicate possible Taliban fighters in the area. About this time I was thinking that the fighters were long gone and we were still out there in hostile land, single ship. We made one more gun run and then told Dog 37 that we hadn't seen anybody. Their response was, "Roger that, be advised the General says you need to come back right now, you aren't supposed to be out there single ship". Apparently someone had told the General everyone on the net heard him clear us to go out single ship, and brought up the fact if anything happened to us, he would be held responsible.

After shooting only a few rockets and a few bullets we headed back to FOB Asadabad. After we landed, a soldier ran up to my aircraft and asked if I needed fuel or ammunition. I told him no then the radio came alive with the controller telling me the General had authorized "his" Blackhawk to follow me back to the same location and continue the fight. Also, the controller stated he had just received a message saying our last gunshot was real close to the attackers. They are holed up in a cave and we almost got them on our last gun run before being called back. Allen and I confirmed with each other where the last location was.

So off we went, with a UH-60 Blackhawk in tow, so as to be "legal" in-country, and not going single ship.

We got in contact with Dog 37 again and they confirmed what had been told to us a few minutes ago, so we continued flying over the ridgeline looking for the attackers. We saw a lot of telltale signs of small caves, like water bottles, food, and trash lying around. We continued the "Recon by fire" strategy by shooting areas that looked like there might be some hiding places. On one pass I saw fresh trash and a small cave. I asked Allen if he saw it also. When he said no, I told him on the next pass I would put the area out the left window and fire a burst of 30mm at it. I lined up my eyesight and the gun onto the location and squeezed off a 10 round burst of 30 mm. I was squeezing off another burst when the gun stopped firing on its own. We both assumed the gun was outside of its safe maneuver limits, and the safety system automatically interrupted the firing. I turned back around and attempted another burst, but that didn't work. Allen said he could hear the gun loader moving as I was squeezing the trigger. I told him to take the gun and try it himself. He tried to fire the gun from his position, in the front seat, and had the same results. The gun just motored with no rounds being fired. We both thought, since we had only fired less than 120 bullets, surely the gun was broken. As we headed back to Asadabad we discussed the possibility of the gun being broken, which is not a good thought. The guns had been working really well all year long, and it wasn't until the last few months that they were starting to show wear and tear from all the shooting we had been doing.

Once again, after we landed, a soldier asked if we needed fuel. I told him no, but asked if he could check our gun to see if we were just out of bullets, or if he could tell if the gun was broken. He just shrugged his shoulders and gave me an "I don't know" look. Allen said he would jump out and check the gun himself. I looked at the soldier and told him I needed some more rockets. He turned around and ran off to get some rockets for us. After Allen checked out the gun, he climbed back into the aircraft and told me we were just out of bullets. That was good news, the gun was not broken so all we had to do was fill it back up.

I was still sitting in the aircraft, with the engines running at a 100%, when the soldier ran back with a High Explosive (HE) rocket in his hands. He gave me this look, like a kid with a really cool toy he wanted me to admire. So I gave him hand signals to place the HE rocket in the "A" zone of the rocket pod, and he gave me that confused look again. So I tried to tell him with some semblance of sign language, to put it in the outer ring of the rocket pod. He shook his head up and down in an "I understand now" motion and proceeded to place the rocket in the front of the pod "pointy end" first! In other words, BACKWARDS! I started banging on the canopy to get his attention when Allen said he would get out and supervise the reloading.

After the Forward Area Rearm Refuel Point (FARRP) guys had brought boxes of 30mm bullets to our aircraft, we discovered they no longer had an up-loader/down-loader, at this FOB. This is a special piece of equipment that is mandatory for rearming the Apache. This was also when I found out that a trained and qualified armament person had left this FOB a week ago. Unknown to us, the previous week an untrained soldier had tried to load up another Apache. He did some serious damage to the gun system, and grounded a perfectly good Apache for several days. As punishment, Idaho National guard (whose aircraft and equipment we were using) took the equipment away, which included their properly trained armament person.

You can't load the 30mm cannon in an "A" model Apache without this piece of equipment. As was obvious, if the person trying to load the gun is not properly trained, or doesn't know what they're doing, they can seriously damage the aircraft.

So, still no problem, or so I thought. I figured I would just let the FOB know we would fly south to Jalalabad (about 30 minutes), and have our own guys rearm us there. We could make the flight down there, reload/refuel, and be back within an hour.

Meanwhile I still couldn't figure out how we only had 140 or so bullets in the aircraft when we launched from Bagram. The Apache was originally designed to carry 1200 bullets. Well, the Army decided to replace the original ammunition pack with a combination fuel cell/ammunition pack that would hold an extra 100 gallons of fuel, but reduce the bullet load to only 330 bullets total.

The only way to know how many bullets were in the aircraft was for the rearming guys to keep track of how many they loaded up. Then a soldier sets the rounds counter manually to that number, and we see it in our displays in the aircraft. When we preflight, all we can visually see is about 60 bullets on the carrier chain before the chain disappears within the aircraft. Throughout the year I only had 2 or 3 fights where I was concerned about running out of bullets and the extra fuel was always a nice thing to have. Having 140 bullets on takeoff that morning, instead of 330, would have been maybe a 1-2% difference in hover power, but since we picked up the mission at the last second and were rushed to get going, I didn't notice the difference in power. Plus, when we did our "gun check", the gun shot fine. The rounds counter was never set upon takeoff and it reset to zero upon shutdown.

Right about this time the TOC called us on the radio and asked if we were ready to go to the KOP. I quickly got on the radio and told them we had no bullets.

I had that really bad feeling again. The TOC called and asked, "Don't you have rockets and missiles?" I responded with, "Yes, but we have no bullets!" Apparently no one seemed to understand the seriousness of going into the Korengal Valley without any bullets. Once again the TOC called back and said that the TIC is over, (we ended up killing 3 insurgents) and the "CODE" (the General) was ready to go to the KOP. Once again I said that we had no bullets, as I watched the "code" getting into the lead Blackhawk.

This is when Arc Angel 32, the lead Blackhawk, got on the radio and asked if I wouldn't mind leading him to the KOP, since he had never been there before. That one statement totally threw me. How could someone not know where the KOP was? We had been going there and getting shot at all year! As I was trying to figure that out, Angel 32 said he would follow me, that way "I could shoot those caves again on the way in". Somehow, I agreed. This is when my bad feeling got worse.

I was not in the initial briefing.

+

I got thrown into the mission at the last second.

+

I flew out single ship.

+

I found out we never had a full load of 30mm bullets.

+

FARRP personnel didn't know how to load up an Apache.

+

I was now **leading** the Blackhawk into the Korengal Valley.

=

Nothing good.

But there I was, heading into the Korengal Valley with a Blackhawk that had never been there, and my aircraft with no bullets. As we flew by the original TIC sight, the ridgeline was covered in white smoke from a "fire mission" shot from Camp Blessing, which was a few miles further west up the Pech River Valley. We continued on, in route to the mouth of the Korengal valley.

As we entered the valley, Allen and I were still discussing what a bad idea it was to go there without any bullets. Allen said he was going to action the gun, in hopes of keeping the bad guys thinking that since the gun was moving around with his head, surely we must have bullets, and therefore, they would not shoot at us.

We made our way southbound into the Korengal Valley and started seeing all of the snow, which had accumulated over the past week, about midway up the mountains. I was still thinking out loud to Allen how it was a really bad idea going into the valley without any bullets for our primary weapon. My stomach was really tightening up now. I couldn't believe what was unfolding.

I made radio contact with the Korengal Outpost, a.k.a. Lumberyard, KOP, Combat main and Attack main, about 2 miles from them. I flew directly over the landing zone and told them that we were inbound with "the Code".

Apaches never land at the KOP. We circle overhead, as the Blackhawks or Chinooks land and drop off or pick up troops and supplies. We set up an orbit so we can deter the enemy from shooting at the aircraft on the LZ, and/or start shooting at known enemy locations if needed.

After I made my initial contact with the lumberyard, I asked them if they had any coordinates for us to look at, while we circle overhead waiting for the Blackhawk to do its business. This is standard operating procedure. Sometimes it would take several minutes for the aircraft to offload or upload. This would give us time to put in coordinates into the computer, and check out some areas of interest for the soldiers on the ground.

While Arc Angel 32 was sitting on the LZ unloading his payload, Allen and I discussed getting back to Jalalabad to get bullets while we waited for the time to pick up the "Code". We knew the General was supposed to spend a few hours on the ground. We were planning on going straight back to Jalalabad to have our guys load bullets, rockets, and fuel to get us through the rest of the day.

As we made our second lap around the LZ, Arc Angel called us on the radio and asked if we wouldn't mind leading them back out of there. This is when I got fed up with the nonsense. I told him, "No, you can lead us out of here, because I can cover you better from behind. It was SOP anyway, and there wasn't anything I could do with those caves that we had shot up earlier!" We couldn't see the caves because of all the smoke from the previous fire mission.

Unknown to Allen and me, at that moment, the KOP and Arc Angel were being fired upon. It was told to me later, someone ran up to the pilots in the Blackhawk and told them to get out because they were under attack. So, Arc Angel 32 did what he thought was right, he took off. Problem was he left his crew chief/door gunner running for cover, while under fire on the LZ, with the package and the general.

Allen and I were just southeast of the LZ, northbound, when we saw Arc Angel takeoff from the LZ heading south. I told Allen over the intercom, "There they go ". Arc Angel took off to the south and continued his flight southbound out of the KOP, flying low and slow.

Right then, the LZ controller, on the KOP, got on the radio and stated, "Egress to the north, egress to the North", with a real sense of urgency in his voice.

The Korengal valley is a north-south valley, and the KOP sits on the western side of it. The valley is only about 5 miles long and would be better called a box canyon by the pilots who fly there. It's extremely rugged, steep, and the bottom is at 6500 ft above sea level. The surrounding mountains that make up the valley rise over 12,000 ft.

We had learned earlier in the year that trying to depart from the KOP and fly south to cross over the lowest point of the surrounding mountains, required us to coax our aircraft to climb over 6000 feet in less than 3 miles. Couple that with the fact that we usually were operating at the max limitations of our aircraft, both aerodynamically and engine performance wise, we get shot up. We were sitting ducks climbing out the south end of the Korengal Valley. The main villages in the valley were at the south end, so there was no surprising the Taliban when we tried flying out that way. No one flies out the south end of the valley if they know what's good for them. Also, everything on the east side of the valley is bad news. It is the ridgeline that abuts the Shuriyak Valley, which is the entrance to the valley where we had the previous shooting at the caves.

Arc Angel 32 departed the LZ, and was headed Southbound out of the KOP, low and slow. I was east of him, headed north, waiting for him to make a left turn back northbound. I planned on making a left turn, slide in behind him, and fly out northbound as fast as possible.

So when the ground controller made that radio call, "Egress to the north, egress to the north", I was puzzled as to why he would say that. I called back and told him, "Yeah, both Deadwood and Arc Angel will be egressing to the north this time". Meanwhile, I was thinking to myself, why would he ask that? I looked out my left canopy at Arc Angel and started my left turn over the KOP. I mumble to Allen over the ICS, "Well I hope they start turning. Come on bubba start your turn". Arc Angel continued his flight southbound, low and slow and called me to ask, "Hey Deadwood, where you guys at?" I quickly called him and told him, "I'm high to your right 5 o'clock. Go ahead and start your left turn now!"

Arc Angel called back, "roger that, I'm passing smoke out my left door right now, possible POO sight" (Point Of Origin). Basically, he was getting shot at by the Taliban who just started their attack from the south side of the KOP. He continued his flight low and slow southbound directly towards a known Taliban village.

I told him "don't go any farther south, start your left turn now!" with as much urgency as I could muster, without yelling at him over the radio. He finally started his left turn at the bottom of the valley right over the village. I told him one more time, "Pick up your speed as fast as you can. This is really not good being here!"

Allen and I were still much higher than Arc Angel, at his 5 o'clock position, when he finally turned northbound. I continued following him from that position. We were still trying to figure out where all the smoke was coming from and I had a really bad feeling about the whole situation.

We headed northbound and the sun was just rising over the ridgeline to my right. Arc Angel continued northbound at the bottom of the valley and then started to turn to the right, up a small ridgeline running from the eastside. At this point, Arc Angel was almost back at the KOP. He had basically flown south for about a mile and did a 180 turn and was climbing slowly towards me. Allen and I were looking at Arc Angel, wondering where the previous POO sight was that Arc Angel (AA) had called out. Allen said he saw some smoke at our 11 o'clock. I was still keeping an eye on Arc Angel as he slowly started climbing and turning towards me.

As I looked at the right side of the Blackhawk I caught, what I thought to be, a glint of sunshine shining off of his main rotor mast. What I saw next was absolutely shocking. The "glint" that I thought I saw, was actually an RPG fired from the left side of AA. It had passed right between the body of the Blackhawk and the Main rotor blades, towards me. With that shot, there was an eruption of fully automatic gunfire directed at both sides of Arc Angel. I then witnessed another RPG, fired from his right side, pass underneath him, and then impact the opposite side of the valley. I called out to Allen, "Oh, what was that?"

When I realized what I was witnessing, I called out, "There they are!" referring to the Taliban on both sides of Arc Angel, unloading everything they had at him. Knowing I didn't have any 30mm bullets, I made a hard roll to the left and dove at the group of Taliban still shooting at the tail end of Arc Angel, as he was still slowly flying away to the North. I tried like hell to line up the nose of my Apache to get off some rockets and get these guys, while at the same time making sure I didn't smack the ground. When I realized that I was way too close to make a rocket shot, I continued driving down at the Taliban (who were still shooting at AA) in an effort to draw the intense gunfire away from the Blackhawk. I literally thought I was going to see Arc Angel explode in front of me, that's how much gunfire was directed at them. As I flew directly over the Taliban, I told myself, out loud, "SHIT", because I knew I had just witnessed the possible shoot down of the Blackhawk I was assigned to protect. I also realized that there was no way I could fire off a rocket at these insurgents. Just on the other side of the ridgeline was the KOP. I knew it was too tight to try and squeeze off a rocket, and either hit the insurgents or overshoot, and hit our own FOB.

I drove the aircraft straight at the insurgents and I could see them still shooting at Arc Angel. It seemed all at once they realized there was an Apache coming straight at them from out of the sun. They did exactly what I wanted them to do; they stopped shooting at the Blackhawk and tried swinging their weapons as fast as they could at my Apache helicopter, swooping in on them low and fast.

I called Arc Angel and told them to continue flying north out of the valley because I was making a left turn to engage the fighters who had just attacked them.

I made a max effort turn to the left and called the Korengal Outpost, which was pretty much directly underneath me. I asked Combat Main if they had anyone (American friendlies) in the area. I pretty much knew there were no Americans on that ridgeline shooting at us, but I at least had to make an honest effort to make sure I was not about to shoot up friendly forces.

I received no response, but that was fine because I was on a mission. I continued my left turn to line up the nose of my Apache at the ridgeline that the gunfire had just come from. I told Allen that was where I thought they were.

In that moment, I went into, what we refer to as, "time compression".

Most people have felt this when they experience something so unbelievable that time seems to slow down. When someone remembers what happened in an event, they remember vivid details, their vision becomes razor sharp and it seems that it took forever to play out. In reality the event took just a few seconds from start to finish. The first time I could remember this happening to me, was in my crash back in 1995.

As I lined up my attack symbology in my helmet mounted display, I noticed something peculiar all around my canopy. I then realized I was witnessing bullets whizzing by my canopy. I could literally see the smoke from the bullets as they passed all around. I also saw that telltale signature of gunfire aimed at me by the white muzzle flashes, sparkling in front of me. I saw several strings of large tracers arcing upwards towards me from directly in front and the right side. I thought I was going to see my copilots head explode onto my blast shield right in front of me. Words alone cannot describe the amount of ammunition that was being fired at me!

I then saw a quick flash and a huge puff of ground dust erupt in front of me, followed by a large red object arcing its way towards me, head on. I thought oh shit, it's a missile being fired at me and the belly of the aircraft is where it's going to hit! That was when I performed what I refer to as, "The Matrix Maneuver". I pulled back on the cyclic and climbed up out of the stream of gunfire that was all around me. With the belly of the aircraft exposed to the potential missile I thought, "Shit, this is how it's going to end, a missile shot to the belly of my aircraft."

As people say, my whole life flashed before my eyes. I literally saw my wife and kids faces flash before me. I envisioned what they were going to say when they found out that I had been shot down so close to coming home.

At the same time, I began to figure out how I was going to at least try my best to maneuver my stricken aircraft towards the KOP and make a successful crash landing. All of these thoughts raced through my mind in milliseconds. As I came back to the real world I thought, "This is bullshit! Bad idea! I'm out of here!"

Then I thought, "Nope. I have to show these guys that they can't just randomly shoot at us and get away with it." That's when I switched over from victim mode to Gun Pilot mode. So I pushed forward on the cyclic and started squeezing on the trigger to get a rocket shot off on these guys. I pulled on the trigger, and pushed forward on the cyclic, trying to get the nose of the aircraft lined up on the ridgeline, while not flying into the intended target. I was in a negative "G" dive, which means I was "playing spaceman" or in layman's terms, in zero gravity flight.

The Apache has another safety inhibitor built into it that keeps any rockets from being fired unless you have at least a half positive G on the airframe. I found out later, from the accelerometer in the aircraft, that we had pushed close to 1.5 negative G's on this maneuver. That's another great thing about the Apache over the Cobra helicopter; you can get way more maneuverability out of this airframe than you ever could out of the Cobra.

So there I was, committed to an attack run, without any bullets. I was in a negative G pushover/dive, with the enemy blazing away at me with everything they could muster and I was squeezing the trigger, muttering, "fuck, fuck, fuck" each time trying to coax the aircraft to fire just one rocket.

Just as I was about to pull out of my attack run, I finally got the Apache within ½ a positive G, and one rocket shot out of the rocket pod. It streaked ahead and left a smoke trail as it slammed into the ridgeline right where the insurgent was standing among a group of his cohorts firing at me.

I made a hard left turn and started calling the Lumberyard on the radio to make sure they were watching, and hopefully, covering my attack run. As I was calling, I reached over and started pushing the manual flare dispensing button for the CMWS (pronounced C-MOSS) on the cyclic. I unintentionally stopped pushing the radio call rocker switch mid sentence, while I used the same thumb to release flares to cover my ass on the out bound portion of the attack. I definitely didn't want to have a heat seeking missile come up from behind, while I exited out of the attack run.

There was only so much room in the Korengal Valley before I reached the other side and had to start my turn away from the opposite canyon wall. I elected to turn back left to make another attack because I was thoroughly pissed at that point, and payback was on my mind.

I was so intent on making the turn as quickly as possible, that I pushed too much left pedal and made the turn quicker, but totally out of "trim". In other words, I skidded the tail of the helicopter to the outside of the turn.

This is another safety feature of the Apache. If you are out of trim, the rockets will not fire, no matter how many times or how hard you squeeze the trigger. I lined up with the ridgeline and started squeezing the trigger. Once again, nothing was coming out of the rocket pods. I muttered out loud with frustration in my voice, "Come on, come on!" That's when I realized I was way out of trim and eased off on my left pedal to bring the Apache back into trim.

I lined up my attack symbology on my helmet display unit in front of my right eye, and started firing high explosive rockets as fast as I could pull the trigger. I also started gently pushing back and forth on the rudder pedals, while shooting, to help disperse the rockets. I had remembered reading about a WWII pilot doing that to make his bullets cover a larger area on his gun runs. Plus, after shooting for almost a year now in combat, we had gotten real precise on our rocket shots. I didn't want all my rockets to impact in the same location. I saw some of the insurgents running down the back side of the ridge and I wanted to make this attack run cover as much of that ridgeline as possible. I could easily hear the thumps of each high explosive rocket impacting through my helmet.

I continued my attack runs for several more passes as I worked each pass a little farther down on the back side of the ridgeline. I ran out of high explosive rockets on the second run and switched over to firing the flechette rockets. After I ran out of those, I switched over to firing the white phosphorous rockets as I covered as much of the area as I could.

As I finished firing all my rockets, I called the Lumberyard and told them, "I am Winchester (out of ammunition) and out of here". I also relayed to them that I had just been engaged by a large caliber automatic weapon with lots of big tracers. I said this with a lot of excitement in my voice, for obvious reasons.

The Lumberyard controller replied, confirming what I had just told him, and he called several of his own outposts to try to engage what enemy, if any, was left in the area.

Right then, Arc Angel called asking if they could come back into the Korengal Valley and pick up their Crew Chief that they had left behind on the LZ. With disbelief, I told them they needed to make sure and check themselves for damage, and I no longer had any ammunition to cover them. I also told them a "fire mission" was most likely about to begin on the ridgeline. Arc Angel called back saying they knew they took some hits because they had several systems not functioning in their aircraft, but they were still flyable. I told them to continue flying to FOB Asadabad and I would link up with them as I came out of the Korengal valley.

As we reached the mouth of the Korengal valley, I made visual contact with Arc Angel. We let them know to continue flying on to Asadabad and we would catch up to them and follow behind.

That is when Allen and I finally took a deep breath, and what just happened a few moments ago started to sink in. It was all I could do to keep from going crazy I wanted to just scream out in frustration. The whole day never should have happened, and it still wasn't over. I started going over how "if only we had bullets" and "how could I have been so naïve". I knew better than to go into that valley without bullets!

Apparently, word had spread very fast throughout Afghanistan about what happened. A few minutes later, when we landed at FOB Asadabad, one of our Armament technicians was waiting for us. He had an up loader/down loader ready to refill us with 30 mm. He also had an entire platoon of soldiers ready to help him load us up with rockets and refuel us. They had also contacted the quick reactionary force (QRF) Apaches from Jalalabad. The 2 QRF Apaches were passing by us, in route to the Korengal, as we were getting re-armed and refueled.

We had stirred up a real hornet's nest on this deal.

Allen and I remained in our aircraft as the swarm of enlisted soldiers checked us over for any damage and reloaded our rockets, gun and fuel. When we were back up to 100%, we received radio traffic telling us to get ready to launch back into the Korengal Valley and pick up the Code. Apparently the Code was not going to stay "several hours" as planned earlier. The other Blackhawk was spooled up and ready to go, I knew the Captain who was the pilot in command (PIC) of that aircraft. He was a no-nonsense kind of guy and had been to the Korengal all year. Unlike the previous crew, this Blackhawk pilot knew how to get in and out of the KOP with a minimum amount of B.S.

The armament sergeant from Jalalabad got on the intercom attached to the wing of my Apache and told us we were all loaded up with rockets, bullets, and full of gas. He also reassured us we had no damage to the aircraft. Basically we were ready to go back to the valley.

I had started winding down from the previous hour's worth of excitement and was thinking about how we would fly back into the Korengal, pickup the Code, and then get out with as little excitement as possible. Camp Blessing had already fired up several artillery missions and our 2 QRF Apaches were already in the valley looking for any signs of the Taliban wanting to fight.

The new Arc Angel and I departed FOB Asadabad in route to the Korengal Valley. As we passed the previous cave hunt, DOG 37 called to ask if we could mark the cave sight again and pass them the coordinates. Arc

Angel and I decided that he would hold on the north side of the Pech river valley while I flew over the cave site's to get the coordinates.

As I flew over the location, I spotted some caves that I had not seen earlier and asked Allen if he had seen them as well. He wasn't sure if he was looking at the same caves that I pointed out, so I shot some 30mm into one of them to make sure. It was a great feeling when I squeezed my trigger and that reassuring sound of our gun shook the aircraft and pounded the entrance to that cave sight.

There were plastic milk containers that the Taliban used to hold their water and some plastic bags lying around that they used to carry food. We got the coordinates and passed them on to Dog 37. We then continued on to the Korengal Valley, about two miles up the Pech river valley.

As we flew on to the entrance of the valley, Arc Angel called me on the radio and said he would pass me on my left side so he could take up the lead, as briefed beforehand. I started slowing down a bit so he could pass me up, but as I looked out my left side I still couldn't see him, which worried me because we were already at the entrance to the valley. I wanted him to get ahead of me so I could keep tabs on him, but most of all, we both needed to start picking up our speed. I had already experienced what happens when you go slowly in the valley; you're a sitting duck for the Taliban to take shots at you.

Finally, Arc Angel passed me as he picked up speed and started gaining altitude heading directly for the KOP. This was a good sign. This Captain knew what he was doing, and wasn't messing around. It's always a good, reassuring feeling flying with another experienced aviator.

As we rounded the last ridgeline before seeing the Lumberyard, the radios came to life with the 2 QRF Apaches flying around the south end of the Korengal Valley. They were looking for any sign of the insurgents that had been shooting at us a few hours earlier. Arc Angel was landing, and I was making my first orbit around the KOP. I started making a radio call to those 2 Apache's, but I was cut short by Arc Angel, as he was already departing from the KOP. Again, this was a good sign. Arc Angel landed, loaded his cargo, and departed in seconds. He made a hard left turn over the KOP and added max power to get out of there as fast as he could. I would imagine "the Code" had something to do with that also. I was in perfect position to start a dive and add max power to get the maximum acceleration out of my Apache and I caught Arc Angel in no time at all. I looked at my airspeed indicator and saw 190 knots airspeed build up easily in seconds.

I called back to our QRF Apaches and had them follow us out of the valley. As we made a right turn, east bound, into the Pech river valley, I called our 2 trail Apaches and let them know I would show them the cave sights we had shot at earlier. Camp Blessing, 3 miles west of us in the valley, had fired a salvo of white phosphorous artillery shells at the cave riddled ridgeline, but the west breeze had moved the entire white smoke cloud to the opposite side ridgeline. I told the 2 QRF Apaches I would fire 2 white phosphorous rockets at the correct ridgeline and mark the caves for them.

I was still doing over 140 knots when I lined up my symbology in my helmet display unit. I squeezed off a rocket and the first rocket hit a little high on the ridgeline as it made that familiar white cloud explosion. I then lined up to fire a second rocket at the lower/closer portion of the ridgeline. This time when the rocket hit, it also made that familiar white starburst explosion, but several of the exploding streamers came right at my aircraft. No problem. I made a hard left turn, loaded up some G's, and avoided getting some of the incendiary remnants on my aircraft. I leveled out of my turn, called the 2 QRF Apaches, and told them to look in that area for more caves.

Once again, I added max power to catch up to Arc Angel who had continued his eastward flight towards FOB Asadabad. We had enough fuel to make it all the way back to Bagram, so we just bypassed Asadabad and made our 1 hour flight home.

The rest of the flight and landing were normal. Once on the ground at Bagram, it was apparent that the whole base had heard of that day's events. What was even more revealing was the video that I had gotten with my camera.

We set up a make shift theater in our hooch and started watching all that was recorded. I was doing that "Pilot Thing", trying to explain the day's events and how things had unfolded, and almost ended, to all the other pilots and enlisted guys. I was doing this with some of the best "hand flying" that any combat pilot would have been proud of. When the portion of the video got to the actual missile I thought was going to take me down, things got very quite in the room full of seasoned gun pilots. You could see the bullets and several explosions underneath my aircraft and you could definitely tell by the tone of my voice, things got really wicked, really fast.

Watching the video was no big deal but what really sent chills down my spine was listening to the sounds of the attack and the tone in my voice.

It seemed as if the day was lasting on and on. The Blackhawk "A" company senior instructor pilot came by later to ask what happened. He heard there was video evidence of one of his pilot's actions that got one of his aircraft shot up and nearly cost some lives. I talked to him for a few moments, explaining what happened, and he advised me the pilot had not been to the Korengal all year long. We both looked at each other knowing we nearly had a major screw up, and came very close to losing some American lives because of this.

I then showed him the video. As we were watching it, I was explaining what I was thinking and my concerns. He couldn't believe what was unfolding before his eyes. After watching most of the highlights of the video, he asked me if I wouldn't mind briefing his pilots and crew chiefs on what I had experienced that day. I told him sure. We all needed to learn from this, and hopefully prevent it from ever happening again.

It was 2 days later and I was standing before the Alpha company pilots and crew chiefs. I stood there and looked at them, and that's when I realized how old I was and how young those kids were. They were all quiet and looking at me like I was some sort of senior commander or something. After their standardization instructor pilot (SIP) briefed them on his take of the day's events, he handed me the remote to the video player.

I looked at the kids and started telling them what had transpired and what I thought went wrong, but I fell short of words that fully described what could have happened, so I commenced to play the video. I only played the tape from when I was leading the Blackhawk into the Korengal Valley and then just pointed out what was not obvious in the video.

When we got to the point where the shooting started, you could have heard a pin drop in that room. I played the video for a few more moments where it showed my attack on the ridgeline, but it was more than obvious that we came very close to losing an aircraft with everyone onboard. There were lots of muffled "ooh's" and "oh shits" in the room that evening.

Everyone looked at the Blackhawk pilot and wondered what he could have been thinking, doing what he did. It was finally time for him to tell his side of the story. He tried his best to make it sound like he knew what he was doing, but it was more than obvious that his cohorts weren't buying into his story.

We finished up and I walked out of their company area wondering what I would have said to his friends and family if things had gone totally wrong. I then started thinking about myself and how my wife and children would have reacted if I had been shot down and never came home. Or worse yet, what if Allen had gotten hurt when I made my attack run's. So many scenarios played out about what ifs and none had a pretty outcome.

2 days later I was having lunch with the Arizona boys who were just showing up to relieve us within the next few weeks. We grabbed our food and tried to find a spot to sit. For whatever reason, that day the chow hall was full. We finally found a table near the back and made a beeline for the open seats. After we sat down, I started telling them about the Korengal Valley and about the other hot spots that they should take extra care flying in. As I was talking about the shootings we had all year in the Korengal, the person next to me blurted out that he knew about how bad the valley was personally. I didn't turn around to look at him right away because I was thinking he was some person that maybe had been there once or heard about it, and figured he knew all about it. When I did turn around I saw that he was a One Star General. I quickly glanced at his name tape and sure enough it was the general who was on Arc Angel, January 5th.

The General started telling me about the shooting he was in a few days earlier and was trying to impress me with all the events he witnessed. I finally told him that I was the Apache pilot who escorted him in and nearly got shot out of the sky because of him. He made a gesture to his aid and was discreetly handed a Coin. He started telling me about how he had witnessed 3 different locations that were shooting at me as I made my attack runs. He tried impressing me with how they had to run for cover as bullets were flying all over that FOB. He did at least make one statement about how he thought I was going to get shot down due to the heavy volume of RPG's and heavy machine gun fire coming at me. He said there was shooting coming at me from all sides and then mumbled some speech of sorts and proceeded to hand me his coin.

The Army has gotten into this Challenge Coin thing, which I have yet to figure out. Some of these coins are really fancy and big. I have been the recipient of several and have found the ones really worth their weight in gold are the ones that are truly earned in the truest sense of the meaning. They are given by the soldier that really couldn't afford the coin and was giving it with his true feelings of thanks behind it. You can tell when you get one that is given with all their heart.

I accepted his coin and promptly pulled off my Coyote troop patch off my flight suit and handed it to the General and said, "This is the patch that I had on that day of the shooting". The General gave me this look of real thankfulness, because he knew I had given him something directly related to that near fateful day.

===

I had emailed a seriously grainy small portion of the video on our slow internet to my family and friends on my email list. Most of them could not see the RPG, but it was the sound of my voice and my rockets blasting away at that ridgeline that said it all. I came very close to widowing my wife and orphaning my children.

I even had a friend who I worked with write me back, telling me to think about what I send before I send a video like that. Listening and watching that video sent chills down his back, and he is an O-6 Navy commander who flew attack aircraft off of carriers. He was concerned about my wife and how she would respond to seeing her husband in real combat on the other side of the world.

I had less than a week of flying left, and then it would be time to start packing up and getting ready to go home. I was pretty much spent after a year of combat and being away from my wife and children. I was more than ready to come home.

Finally got the aircraft within half a positive G, and fired one rocket at insurgent. January 5 2007 KOP shoot.

Shooting at the caves, in search of the insurgents,
in support of Dog 37.

Chapter 11

Answered Prayers

Lisa *His time to come home for good was always up in the air. The day kept getting changed which was very irritating. Every day I was getting different information than what had been previously told to me. It was extremely hard to plan anything. Then add to it the time change, which made it even harder. We were always on edge, because we just didn't know. I wanted everything to be perfect, including the yard when he came home, because he was always particular about the yard. I was running around like a wild woman trying to make sure everything was perfect. I rushed around to make sure everything was in place, so he wouldn't have any stress or any worries when he got home. The day finally came, and I took the kids out of school and we drove up there with his parents. The atmosphere at the base was full of energy and anticipation. I'd never seen so many happy and excited people in one place before.*

It was unbelievable to me when I was packing all of my belongings in preparation to go home for good. One year had gone by faster than I ever expected it would, yet at times it dragged on. I started placing the pictures of my kids and wife and all the drawings and letters that school kids had sent me in a big plastic container I was going to ship home.

I sat down on my makeshift chair and recalled the routine that I had done every morning. Wake up before the sun, check my e-mail, and then head down to the command post to find out my mission for the day. Before leaving my room I would make sure my computer was turned off and my letter was placed on top of it.

I had written a letter to my wife and kids telling them my last thoughts and wishes. I left it on top of my computer in case something happened to me and I wasn't returning home. It was already addressed and ready to mail out with a small post-it note on top. After I placed the letter on top of the computer and made sure everything else was turned off, I would step to my door, stop, and before closing and locking it, I would quickly say a prayer. I would then visualize in my mind, "This is how someone will find my room, if I don't come back." I don't know if any of the other pilots were doing the same ritual, but this was mine, and as I reflected back on the year, I realized that I had done this every day.

The first few times I started my routine, I thought it was a bit morbid, but continuing it every day, it became nothing to think that this could be my last day to live. In the beginning, I kept thinking it could never happen to me, but after the loss of Colossal 3-1 and Tim, and especially after my crash 11 years earlier, I knew when all was said and done, I was mortal, like everybody else.

The last two weeks of my flying were standard Ring Route missions with one of the Arizona National Guard Longbow's flying along. I was constantly stressing to them the importance of not becoming complacent, and if they were assigned to a mission into the Korengal Valley, they were to brief everyone in every aircraft to not hesitate to shoot. They had to know to never take it for granted that everyone will do the right thing once the shooting starts.

And then it happened, just like that, I finished my last flight in Afghanistan. There was no fanfare, no parades, nothing but the sound of the APU shutting down and the ICS going silent as I turned off the battery switch. I grabbed my flight gear, my weapon, and walked across steel beach for the last time to our command post. I turned on the aircraft laptop and started filling out the flight's paperwork. After I finished, I placed my M4 in the arms locker and walked back to my Hooch.

Around the entire base there were new faces at the chow halls and the PX's. The 82nd airborne had arrived to replace us. 10th Mountain division was on pins and needles waiting to find out if they were to be extended for another six months. We had also gotten word the Army was thinking of keeping us there for another six months. I didn't think too much about it because being in the Army Reserves, it would literally take an act of Congress for the Army to extend our tours past one year. I felt bad for the 10th Mountain Infantry guys that had already been extended with less than a month left in their tour. I couldn't imagine having the end so close, and then finding out I was ordered to stay another six months.

It took about a week for everyone to find out who had been extended. The 10th Mountain Aviation Battalion, along with us; were going home as planned.

I let out a sigh of relief, but for some reason I felt I needed to stay longer. I had just spent a year dedicating my life to supporting all those infantry guys that needed our help but I knew I had to go home. My family, my job, and the rest of my life were waiting for me.

I felt guilty knowing that I was going home while the guys I fought alongside with all year had to stay longer. I could only hope the knowledge I imparted to our replacements would continue to serve the 10th Mountain Infantry after I left.

Lisa and I had already made plans and payments to take the family skiing and dog sledding in Colorado. I had to make sure I remained focused on staying safe and going home.

I didn't have too much to pack since I had shipped a lot home over the previous weeks. It was early in the evening and I made my way to the elevated observation deck next to our hooch. I walked up the steps and started looking around the entire base. Being so busy all year, I rarely had the opportunity to come up to the observation deck and just sit down, relax, and enjoy the view. I sat there looking around at all the activity on the flight line barely 50 feet away, and the mountains surrounding Bagram and all the snow that was still covering them. The sun was going down and started shining on the mountains to the east, displaying the Alpenglow. I was thinking about everything that had happened all year.

The country was definitely beautiful, as long as you weren't getting shot at. I thought about the rich history of Afghanistan and how fortunate I was to have been able to fly and see different parts of it. I thought, again, about all the soldiers that lost their lives the past year and I could not imagine how their families were coping with the loss.

Tim came to mind and although I knew him for only a short time, he was one of those individuals that you could talk to for 15 minutes, and afterwards, know you had a friend for life. I will always miss him.

The loss of Colossal 3-1 and its entire crew also still weighed on my mind. I couldn't help but think if I would've been the one providing cover for them; the outcome might have been completely different.

I remembered when we first showed up the comment made to us by the pilots we were relieving. I vividly remembered one of them telling us, "There is nothing going on in this country. We only had two shootings all year long. Enjoy the flying and have a good time."

Yeah right.

I couldn't even begin to remember how many shootings I had gone through all year long.

One thing's for sure; the only time I was ever anxious about actual combat was when I was thinking about what might happen. Once in the cockpit, flying, it was all business. I had no time to be anxious or worried, just like the Vietnam era instructors taught me in flight school, training made all the difference in the world. Once the shooting started, training kicked in, and I accomplished the task without even thinking about it.

When I was home on my mid tour break, several people asked me if I was ever scared getting shot at, or how I knew if I was shooting at the right people. I told them I knew I was shooting at the right people because I could see them shooting at me first. Actual combat and shooting is so dynamic and happens so fast I didn't have time to be scared. My driving force was knowing the enemy was determined to kill me and the soldiers I was supporting on the ground.

I had a clear conscience.

I knew that every shooting I had gotten into, was righteous. I had no regrets that those humans I killed were combatants and deserved what they got. As far as I knew, I had not shot any innocent civilians.

As I watched the sun go down, the temperatures plummeted along with it.

The next day I was finishing cleaning my room and preparing it for whoever was going to have it next. One of the lieutenants came to my door and told me we were all requested by the 10th Mountain Brigade commander, Colonel Starr, to meet him at his command post. I had only seen him once at the beginning of my tour.

All of the other Apache pilots and I gathered together and made our way to the headquarters building. As we walked along the dusty streets, we all wondered why the Colonel wanted to see us. The lieutenant said Col. Starr was going to present us with a 10th Mountain Brigade coin.

I had just received a coin from the Secretary of Defense Robert Gates two weeks prior since I was one of two Apaches that had escorted his flight to the Pakistani border, so getting a coin from the 10th Mountain brigade was really nothing special, or so I thought.

We were all lined up around the walls of the main briefing room within the brigade headquarters building. After a few minutes, Colonel Starr's aide walked in the room and told us to get ready, the Colonel was right behind him.

171

As Colonel Starr entered the room our captain had us all come to attention by calling out, "Attention! Brigade Commander!"

Colonel Starr immediately told us all, "At ease" as he stopped and looked around the room at each of us.

He began by telling us he was sorry that he did not get to talk to us individually throughout the year. He asked us to understand he was very busy running an aviation brigade in a war zone. He then asked us if we knew how much good we had done throughout the year.

He told us of all the intelligence reports he received saying the Taliban and Al Qaeda were scared of us, and had called off numerous attacks whenever we showed up in the area. There was no telling how many soldiers and aircraft we saved just by being present. He went on to say he had also received numerous reports from ground commanders asking him to, "Thank you Apache guys for doing your mission." Colonel Starr was walking slowly around the room, looking at each one of us, as he was telling us all the good that we had done, throughout the year. He then went to the head of the room, stopped, turned around, and began telling us one individual story that brought out exactly how much good we did, and were probably never aware of.

He told us about a Medevac mission in an eastern province along the Pakistan border. A convoy of Humvee's was driving along a lone deserted road and one of them had a soldier riding on top, manning the machine gun. The convoy was ambushed by insurgents shooting RPG's and heavy machine guns and the soldier riding on top was struck by an RPG. It impaled the soldier in his lower abdomen and the RPG itself was protruding out of his hip. The warhead did not detonate.

The convoy successfully maneuvered outside of the kill zone, but was still stranded in the valley with insurgents circling for a final attack. The medevac was called and launched out of Bagram with one of the Apaches as its escort.

When the flight arrived overhead, a translator riding with the ambushed convoy overheard on the radio the Taliban calling for everyone to retreat because there was an Apache in the area. The Blackhawk Medevac was then able to land and pick up the wounded soldier without taking any fire from the Taliban. The soldier was transported to a hospital and after being stabilized, was placed on the first jet transport to Germany.

Colonel Starr went on to say everyone told him the soldier would most likely not survive. And that was all. The Apache pilots continued with their daily missions for the rest of the year. Colonel Starr then walked up to each of us individually as he continued his story. While he was talking, he shook our hand and simultaneously gave us his Brigade coin which was in his palm.

He started choking up as he told us six months after that medevac mission, when he himself had forgotten about it, he received a letter. Enclosed was a picture of the soldier, who we helped evacuate that day, holding his newborn baby and a thank you note to all of us that helped him survive that day, and let him hold his newborn baby. As Colonel Starr shook my hand and gave me the coin, he looked me straight in the eye and I could tell he meant it from the bottom of his soul, he said a sincere thank you for the job we had done for him and his soldiers of the 10th Mountain division.

There was not a dry eye in the room of battle hardened soldiers. That was a coin that was given in the truest sense of its meaning.

==

My only problem now was worrying about getting claustrophobic on my trip home.

I started feeling anxious again thinking about the C-17 flight to Kuwait. I knew the Army needed to rotate an entire battalion of soldiers out of Afghanistan and they didn't care how comfortable we were. They only cared about getting the mission done. If I could just make it to Kuwait without an incident, I could make the rest of the trip without problems.

I still didn't know why I was actually getting these anxiety episodes. I had never been claustrophobic before in my entire life.

I had to make myself concentrate on getting back to my wife, children, and home. I knew if I sat and thought about the flight home, it would only make things worse for me.

Fortunately, for the prior month, I was busy trying to coordinate with a film crew that was being sent by a production company. I was communicating via e-mail with a Los Angeles based production company that was making a segment for a show called "My War Diary". Someone had sent information about the convoy we rescued in the Tagab Valley back in October and the production company, along with the military, was making a program of actual combat operations in Iraq and Afghanistan. They were looking for actual combat video footage and an interesting story that went along with it that they could make a segment with. Trying to coordinate interviews, contracts, and additional footage preoccupied my mind.

Just like the preparation of going home for R&R, the military made us all attend classes and briefings on how to handle ourselves once we were home. The Army was still having problems with soldiers getting into trouble with alcohol, suicide, and spousal abuse, after being away for a year. They seemed to be the only ones having problems with soldiers returning home. All the other services were either not in Afghanistan, or were only there for no more than a few months at a time. I for one can testify being away from home for an entire year is life-changing.

Living a Combat military operational skill (MOS) mindset made things a little more interesting than being the average soldier who never left the safety of the base. As the Preacher told us when we were first departing Fort Hood, the chances of actually being in an all-out shooting fight was supposed to have been slim to none. The fact that all of us were in a shootout, at least once a week for an entire year, definitely had an effect on you, whether you knew it or not. It would just be a matter of time before the effects of this deployment came out.

As the day came to finally board the C-17 to depart Afghanistan, I was too excited to think about any claustrophobia. Although, once we boarded the C-17, I made sure to take a seat on the side of the aircraft as opposed to the seating palettes, which were in the middle. The seating palettes were regular airline seats mounted to an aluminum pallet that could be rolled on, or rolled off easily. The only problem with them was the Air Force mounted the seats with the absolute minimum amount of space in front of each one. To make things even worse, each row was 5 seats wide. I definitely did not want to get stuck in the middle seat, in the middle of a row. That would have been a disaster in the making for me. Although the seats along the side of the aircraft were Spartan at best, I knew I would have space to stretch my legs and stand up if I had to.

Once inside the C-17, I ended up sitting next to a soldier who was also going home. I was talking to him and found out he was with Dog 37, in the Pech River Valley, on January 5th. We spent the better part of the flight talking about the caves that I was shooting up for them on that day. He gave me some pictures of myself, as I flew over them shooting up the insurgents. It was very interesting to see a picture of an Apache shooting and knowing that it was me at the controls.

He also had some pictures of the Taliban that we had killed that day. Without even thinking, I looked at them on his laptop. It surprised me to see one picture of an insurgent I had hit with a white phosphorous rocket. All you could see was a bleached out skeleton, with some semblance of a burned head, hands, and feet with melted sandals. The next picture he showed me wasn't so bad, because I couldn't tell what it was. He explained to me I had hit an insurgent with a high explosive rocket, and if you looked closely you could barely make out bits and pieces of the individual and his clothing. I told him thanks, but I had seen enough. It wasn't that I was getting nauseous at the pictures, it's just I never went into the war dreaming or wishing to kill other human beings. I felt content knowing I saved American lives and I had to take enemy lives to do it. A job is a job.

Kuwait in February was drastically different than in the summer. I could actually walk outside without fear of collapsing from the intense heat that I had felt back in June. We ended up staying in Kuwait for several days until it was our time to make the final flight home.

While in Kuwait I was able to make several phone calls home. I was still on the other side of the world, so I had to time my calls to coincide with my family's schedule, which was going on as normal back home. I couldn't help but notice that the pain in my neck and the tension on my whole body had gone away. I still had pain in my shoulders, but that pain was mainly from my muscles and ligaments that were stressed out from wearing 60 pounds worth of body armor and survival vest, up to 14 hours a day, for an entire year.

It was finally time to board the contract L-1011 for the long journey back to the other side of the world. There were two stops before our final destination, Fort Hood Texas. Our first stop was in Germany. Our route had taken us over the city of Dresden and I looked out the window and thought of the fire bombings that happened during World War II in that city. I realized I was still thinking of war and its ravages as opposed to the beauty of the German countryside below me.

The second stop after Germany was Ireland. While taking a two hour break on the ground in Ireland, I found out our flight would be arriving in Fort Hood the next day. I called up Lisa and told her, the approximate time we would be arriving.

She was making phone calls to my parents, and the other wives whose spouses were deployed with me, to make sure that everyone knew the next and final meeting would be at Fort Hood in 24 hours. Lisa was also coordinating with Shelby and Eric's teachers for time off from school to make sure they were present at my homecoming. Everyone back home was getting excited at the planned reunion of Coyote 29, my call sign in Afghanistan.

==

I was awakened by the flight attendants walking up and down the aisles making sure everybody had their seats up and tray tables stowed. We had one hour left before our final stop.

Lisa, Shelby, Eric, and my parents were all arriving at a gym somewhere in Fort Hood. Everyone in the gym sat down so that they could get briefed by a General and several other dignitaries as to what to expect when the moment came. The gym was filled with families anxiously making final preparations to their signs, banners, balloons, and for the wives, lipstick, make up, and hair touchups, in preparation for the reunion. Shelby was trying to act cool by hiding any feelings she had. After all, she was now an 11-year-old and it just wasn't cool to show any feelings for your dad. Eric was looking around in amazement at all the banners, balloons, and people anxiously awaiting their dad coming home. In Eric's mind, everybody was there for *his* dad.

As the plane taxied to a stop everyone erupted in cheers. I couldn't believe it; we were back in America safe and sound. The airport we landed at didn't have a sky walk, like most major airports. Just like the presidential plane, a truck with a ladder on it, pulled up to the exit door of the jet transport.

Everyone grabbed their belongings, and made their way down the stairway. At the bottom were several commanders and other high-ranking officers, shaking each soldier's hand, and welcoming us home. We made our way across the tarmac to the main terminal building and at the entrance door, a line started forming and backing up. I thought, "Great. I'm finally home and now I have to stand in line, for who knows what."

When the line slowly progressed into the building, I saw what the holdup was. There she was, all 5 foot of her, the "Hugging Lady" was keeping her promise to us.

In the gym, over the PA system, everyone was informed that the aircraft was safely on the ground, barely 5 miles away. The tension in the air was getting thicker and thicker as the time for the reunion was getting closer.

After swiping our ID cards, we made our way out of the terminal to a building across the street. There was another building that had several tables set up to take our weapons and properly secure them. I was amazed at how efficient this process was. Normally signing weapons back into an armory would be an all day process. After turning in our weapons, we went out the back door, and loaded into several busses. Everyone was starting to get excited about finally joining up with our families. I was so excited, that what would have normally been a claustrophobic situation, in the bus, never even entered my mind.

The voice came over the PA system telling all the families the buses were loaded and it would be 15 minutes before they showed up.

The ride in the bus went by quickly. Every intersection we crossed had the local police stopping traffic with their lights on. We pulled into the parking lot outside of the gym that was surrounded by MPs. We all filed out of the buses and established a formation. We could barely make out music and the low roar of voices coming out of the open door to the gym. Once everybody was off the buses and properly lined up in formation, an officer got in front. He told us we would be standing in formation for no more than a few minutes while the dignitaries spoke.

This was it. We started filing in to the gym to the cheering and music from a band. I don't even know what the band was playing because everyone was cheering so loud. Once I entered the gym, I looked to the left and saw banners, balloons, and flags being waved by hundreds of people in the bleachers. I was desperately looking, trying to pick out any one of my family, amongst the standing and waving people.

In the bleachers, Lisa, Shelby, Eric, my mom and dad, were clapping, cheering and waving a banner and desperately trying to pick me out of all the soldiers that had just formed up in front of them.

Standing in formation, I was moving my eyes from left to right, slowly trying to find my family, and then I cracked a huge smile as I saw the banner that Eric was holding.

Eric was holding the banner upside down and didn't realize it.

I wanted to bust out laughing right there.

I looked to either side of Eric and there was my family, cheering, clapping and waving an American flag. A General started speaking on the PA system indicating for everyone to settle down. We all wanted to get it over with. A Chaplain stood up to the microphone and had us all bow our heads for prayer.

177

I don't know how long the prayer lasted; I don't even know who spoke after the chaplain. My eyes were fixed on my family, and as far as I was concerned, there was nobody else in the building. The next words I heard were, "Dismissed!"

It was a free-for-all. Everybody came down off the bleachers while the formation broke up and made direct lines for their loved ones.

The instant chaos reminded me of when a Piñata gets broken and everyone makes a mad dash for the goodies.

Lisa spotted me as I was making my way through the crowd, directly to her. We hugged and kissed each other as tightly as we ever had before.

Once again, I was brought back to reality by the sounds of Shelby and Eric pulling on my uniform saying, "Daaaaad"!

I quickly gave my parents a hug, and then reached down and picked up Eric and hugged him like a teddy bear. As I was hugging Eric, I looked down at Shelby and she was on the verge of crying. I put Eric down and hugged Shelby as she burst into tears of joy. As I was holding her, she told me in my ear, "I knew you would be okay. I knew you would come back. God told me so. Don't ever leave us again!"

My daughter's prayers had come true, just as God had promised her.

Allen and myself on the C-17 flying us to Kuwait for our final journey home, after one year of combat.

Driveway chalk art that Shelby orchestrated for my homecoming.

Finally together after nearly a year apart.

Poster made by Shelby and Eric for my homecoming.

Chapter 12

Moving On

Lisa   *The day he drove home from Ft. Hood he got to town earlier than expected. Our neighbors were putting up ribbons and decorations on their homes, and wanted to be outside when he drove up. He called and said he was an hour early, which normally would have been great news, but I had to tell him to wait, also I had to tell him what the surprise was so he would hold back.*

March 2007, the first week home was a complete blur. After the homecoming in the gymnasium, families were allowed to spend the night off base in a hotel. Finally getting to take a shower in a real bathroom was a long awaited luxury, and it felt as if I had washed off ten pounds, or one year's worth, of dirt and grime. Climbing into a bed with clean sheets, blankets, and pillowcases was another luxury I would never take for granted again. Holding my wife, while lying next to her in bed, was a dream come true. But what brought my mind to ease, as I slowly slipped off to sleep, was the sound of Shelby and Eric giggling as they went to sleep.

It felt as if I had just closed my eyes when I opened them again 10 hours later. I looked around the hotel room and tried to figure out where I was. Lisa, Shelby, and Eric were getting dressed.

After breakfast Lisa dropped me off at base so I could start the process of demobilization. She and my parents drove home, knowing I would be home in a week.

The entire demobilization process was a whirlwind tour of everything that we took care of when we mobilized, over one year ago. Four days had gone by, I was finished with the demobilization, and we were finally released to go home for good. I called Lisa and told her that I would be home in about four hours. She quickly told me I couldn't come home. She didn't know how to keep me away and keep a secret, so she just came right out and told me the plan. Everyone in the neighborhood was planning on

180

lining the streets to wave and cheer me home. If I left at that moment, I would be home before everyone else got off work. I couldn't believe it. I had been gone for 14 months and now I was not allowed to go home. I asked Lisa when would be a good time for me to come home. She told me to start heading that way but to give her a call before I entered our neighborhood.

Six hours later I made the final turn into my neighborhood. I rolled down all of the windows in the car and sure enough, at the first stop sign on the main boulevard there were several groups of families. They were waving signs, American flags, and cheering, welcoming me home. I looked past that first group and saw my neighbors lined up on both sides of the street. I slowly drove down the street thanking each and every one of them. I couldn't believe my eyes. It seemed as if the entire neighborhood had come out to welcome me home.

I made the final turn down my street and every house had a yellow ribbon out front along with an American flag, and some type of sign welcoming me home.

Lined up on both sides of my driveway were the kids from the neighborhood waving flags and cheering. Shelby had taken command of the other kids and orchestrated a huge chalk drawing on my driveway. I parked the car, stepped out and every one of those kids came up to me and welcomed me home. I stayed outside as neighbors drove by honking their horns and welcoming me home. Even my dog, Cowboy, was deep into the moment as he was doing his usual welcome home dance and running around the house at full speed.

I finally stepped inside my home and once again saw all the banners and signs that Shelby and Eric made up for me. Once everything had settled down, Lisa and I embraced each other and said a thank you prayer with Shelby and Eric.

==

I opened my eyes, looked around, and immediately jumped out of bed. "Oh no", I thought, "I'm late for my briefing". I looked around my bed frantically, trying to figure out where I was. It took a few moments for me to realize I was home.

Almost every morning for the next several months, I found myself standing by my bed at four o'clock in the morning after being awakened by a nightmare. I would be drenched in sweat and have to go to the bathroom to get a towel to wipe myself dry. The dreams, and sometimes nightmares, were much too real at times.

I found out later I was not the only one from my unit that was having a hard time making it through an entire night of sleep.

It was very difficult getting back into some semblance of a normal life. Thankfully, a few weeks after coming home, we were taking a family vacation and planning for the trip took my mind further and further away from the war.

Driving to Telluride, Colorado had been our normal family vacation every spring break since Shelby and Eric were born. This time though, as I was driving along, I couldn't help but think about what was going on back in Afghanistan. I desperately wanted to forget about the war and somehow try to bring back some sense of normality to my life but even while skiing and snowboarding, I would catch myself looking around at the mountains and drifting back to the mountains in Afghanistan.

While dogsledding with our friends in Telluride, Mark was one of the first people to ask me what it was like over seas. I told him he wouldn't believe how much combat and shooting we had gone through in one year's time. I wanted to tell him about everything that had happened, but I knew better. I figured the less I thought about the war and the less I talked about it, the quicker I would forget it.

I went back to work at U.S. Custom's, flying a jet and helicopter. A lot of things had changed in the one year time frame I was gone. Several friends had retired and new people had shown up.

Flying a helicopter and jet at work came back naturally. Occasionally, I would see a strobe light or white flash of light from a car windshield and find myself quickly looking at the spot, with anticipation that I would start seeing tracers coming at me from that direction. Even my coworkers noticed I was a little jumpy or on edge when flying around.

A few months after starting work again, I had to take a commercial airline to Washington DC. I had done this quite a few times before, as my job required me to fly to different parts of the country for training or missions. This time things were different. Once I sat down at a window seat in the jet, two other gentlemen sat next to me, essentially blocking me in the row. I looked around and noticed the entire flight was completely full. To top things off, there was a thunderstorm approaching the airport. The airliner taxied out away from the jet way and then came to a stop. The

Captain got on the PA system and informed us we were on hold due to the storm over the airport.

All of a sudden I felt this flush of heat over my entire body and I realized I was trapped inside this plane. The look of sheer panic on my face must have been more than apparent because the two gentlemen sitting next to me asked if I was okay. I told them I couldn't breathe, and was starting to feel very claustrophobic. I was doing my best to try to stay calm, but it was the same feeling I had back in Afghanistan. I'd never felt it before on an airliner, and I normally looked forward to flying on a commercial jet.

Once we were in the air, I calmed down and the rest of the flight was uneventful. A week later when I was flying home, I started feeling claustrophobic again for no apparent reason.

Over the next few months I continued having nightmares and anxiety attacks in claustrophobic situations. I didn't know what was causing all of it but I knew it wasn't right. Eventually I went to the VA and had them look at my shoulder, which I had injured in the crash years ago, and had reinjured in Afghanistan.

The VA sent me to a hospital to have an MRI done. On the day I did my MRI, I was feeling pretty good. The attendant called me into the room and had me lay on the table that was to slide me inside the MRI. I closed my eyes for a second and when I reopened them a huge wave of anxiety came over me. I was reliving the night of my crash and the moment I opened my eyes and found myself inside the MRI machine, I was paralyzed with anxiety. It was the worst claustrophobic situation I ever could have found myself in. All I could do was say a prayer in my head that it would end soon.

I don't remember how long it took, but after that anxiety attack, I felt like I had just run a marathon. I was completely exhausted, both mentally and physically and I was soaked in sweat. I knew then something wasn't right and I needed help.

After talking to a social worker, we realized the beginning of the anxiety attacks was the crash I had back in 1995. Compounding the situation was the loss of friends, and all the shooting I had gone through in combat.

I eventually learned how to deal with the anxiety attacks. They are still with me to this day, although I can control them most of the time. I've learned to recognize situations that could cause claustrophobia, and I do whatever I can to either avoid them, or manipulate the situation in my favor.

Epilogue

Lisa *It was a good thing that I had kids. I couldn't imagine just being a wife, sitting at home alone, wondering and waiting. The kids kept me busy, because they always had something to do. My children are a blessing, and having each other to go through that year together was irreplaceable and priceless.*

Since I've returned from Afghanistan, the war in Iraq has settled down and now there is much more emphasis and news about the Afghanistan war.

The United States Army has abandoned the Korengal Valley. I don't know if it was a decision based on politics or tactics, but at least now I know no more Americans will die in that valley. The media still holds back on a lot of the news that is actually happening in the war. I watch the television intently whenever any video is shown of Afghanistan and I can recognize some of the valleys and Forward Operating Bases that I had flown into. I listen carefully to what they are saying about that specific area, but I take it all in with a grain of salt.

I say prayers for all of our soldiers over there, and I say prayers for the country of Afghanistan as well. It is a beautiful country . . . when they're not shooting at you.

I feel privileged that I got to go to Afghanistan and fly throughout the country. To this day I have no regrets about any of the shootings I had gotten into. I sometimes think about what would have happened or could have happened if I'd done something different in a fight, but in the end, I know deep down, I did my best to protect the soldiers I was fighting along side of.

I also know from the bottom of my heart that God was with me the entire time. I know he protected me from what I could and couldn't see. There were too many fights I had gotten into and came out of without a scratch, wondering how I had escaped getting hit or getting knocked out of the sky.

Daniel Flores

If I was called to go back, I would go immediately, although I hope it never happens. If my country needed me again, I would have no hesitation, whatsoever. I don't know if it's a sense of duty or honor or both. I just know the United States of America is the greatest country in the world and I would do whatever asked to defend it and my family.

44263250R00126

Made in the USA
Lexington, KY
09 July 2019